BE YOUR BEST SELF

Rebekah Ballagh

BE YOUR BEST SELF

TEN LIFE-CHANGING IDEAS TO REACH YOUR FULL POTENTIAL

ALLEN&UNWIN
SYDNEY·MELBOURNE·AUCKLAND·LONDON

CONTENTS

Hi, lovely human!

Welcome!

Introduction

I am so glad you are here. It's time to find your best self — and I'm here to guide you on the journey.

I wanted to take a moment to introduce myself, this book, and to give you a few ideas about how you might like to make the most out of what's inside.

My name is Rebekah Ballagh, but you can call me Becks. I'm a qualified counsellor, a self-development coach, a mindfulness teacher, a mama and a wife . . . a lover of food, hot water bottles, being with family, slow strolls in nature, Netflix binge sessions, fluffy socks, Kmart and spending far too long in the shower. I'm also someone who has a long story of my own involving anxiety, panic attacks, depression and struggles with self-worth and my inner critic.

I've spent years training, taking post-graduate specialist courses, and working on my own self-development. For more than thirteen years I've worked in wellbeing and mental health, helping thousands of clients on their own paths. And I can't wait to share with you a smorgasbord of some of the things I have learnt along the way.

I hope as you read this book you experience some lightbulb moments — when that little bolt of insight or sudden understanding makes you say, 'Aha!' As you explore these pages you might have moments where something just goes 'click!' in your mind, and you get the sense that something profound has just dawned on you. When you have a lightbulb moment, there is huge potential to create change and find your best self. Change starts with awareness. Acknowledgement. A lifting of the veil of what we once believed, in order to see our truth and re-write our stories.

Over the past few years, I have been working with groups online in coaching programmes. During this time we have explored many of the topics that you will find in this book, and there is a common thread to the feedback I have received. The participants so often write to me to tell me that 'suddenly it all makes sense'. They feel seen, normal, validated. They realise nothing is wrong with them. Many point out they spent years in therapy or thousands of dollars on psychologists and counsellors, but it wasn't until they found the information from my programmes — all of which you'll find in this book, and more — that it suddenly clicked and things changed for them. (I don't know how to say this stuff without feeling like I am trying to toot my own horn! It must be that pesky imposter syndrome of mine again. But this isn't about me, and I have certainly never considered myself an expert. I don't have a magic wand — dammit! — but I do have a toolkit of information and things to show you that just may change your life.)

Maybe you are here because you're struggling with self-confidence and you want to discover ways to feel comfortable in your own skin. Maybe you're battling anxiety and worries and want to learn how to be more present in your life. Maybe you feel stuck in a rut, never feeling good enough, and you want to be free from all those old limiting beliefs and critical thoughts about yourself. Maybe you've noticed you have a tendency to hijack your own attempts at growth, becoming stuck in a pattern of self-sabotage and you want to find some genuinely useful tools to get unstuck. Whatever your reason for being here, I trust that you will find lots of incredible tools in this book to help you on your journey.

When I say this book is a smorgasbord, I really mean it. I have collected some of the most life-changing tools and information I have gathered along the years and put together a toolkit of offerings that just might change your life. We're covering everything from your inner critic to perfectionism, self-sabotage and procrastination to the nervous system, limiting beliefs to inner child work, boundaries to self-love. It is all here. There are so many nuggets of pure gold in this book (well . . . I think so, anyway!) and my greatest hope is that you are able to find some pieces that resonate with you and are the catalyst for finding your best self.

Ultimately, I hope that what you take away from all of this is more self-compassion for yourself as you navigate your life. We can be so hard on ourselves. Often we are our own biggest barriers to growth and contentment. I'd like to teach you some of the reasons why that is and, most importantly, how you can change your old unhelpful patterns to create a new way of being in the world, with others and in your relationship with yourself.

In terms of how you might like to use and navigate this book, *Be Your Best Self* is split into ten life-changing ideas to improve your life. Within each of these discoveries, you will find wee treasure chests of chapter topics to make it easy for you to head straight to something you need at any given time.

Many of the chapters lean on and reference one another, scaffolding you into higher learnings and deeper discoveries, so you may like to read the book in order first and then possibly revisit sections that really speak to you or that you feel called to do more work around.

The ten life-changing ideas are:

1. Discover your inner critic
   & inner worth

2. Decode your emotions

3. Step out of the worry trap

4. Break free from self-sabotage

5. Tame your thoughts

6. Re-write your limiting beliefs

7. Let go of what others think

8. Protect your energy

9. Create healthy habits

10. Learn to love yourself

I encourage you to take some time to digest each idea as you navigate them. Do try to stop and pause if there is an exercise you come across in these pages that might benefit you. So often we pick up books like this, read them cover to cover and then sit back wondering why we aren't suddenly a brand new person. 'I read the darn book, so why am I not floating on air and glowing?!'

We will explore all of these barriers and how to change in the chapters ahead — but a disclaimer now, in the very beginning: you need to invest in yourself and your development by setting aside some time to actually put the tools ahead into practice in your life. I also suggest jotting down any of your personal 'aha!' moments — put them on Post-its, and read them daily. Highlight sections that speak to you. Dog-ear the pages! Use this book to its fullest potential and make it your own.

I absolutely believe that each and every person is capable of change and of growth. At my darkest points with anxiety I was having frequent panic attacks, I doubted myself every day, I felt like a failure. I felt down, stuck, overwhelmed . . . and I worked and invested in myself, leaning in and pushing through. I learnt to sit with discomfort. There was a point where having to speak in a room to just two or three people sent me into a panic attack. Now I have been on TV (several times), been a part of numerous live radio interviews, and I run webinars, coach groups and speak to large audiences and organisations regularly. Not only do I love it, I'm good at it. And I have full and complete faith that you too can conquer your goals and feel good in yourself too.

So let's do it. I'm right here with you. Well . . . not literally — that would be weird — but I am here in spirit, cheering you on and patting you on the back the whole way. Thanks for showing up for yourself today. I can't wait for you to see who you can become.

Off you go — time to be your best self!

Becky

@journey_to_wellness_
journeytowellness.online

DISCOVER YOUR INNER CRITIC & INNER WORTH

What better place to start your journey in this book than by getting to know those 'little voices in your head' — the inner critic and your inner coach.

Let's begin by exploring the role your inner critic plays in self-sabotage and low self-worth, then relegate it to the backseat and take back the steering wheel by connecting with your sense of inner worth and compassion.

Your Inner Critic

I stood in front of the mirror, tugging at the uncomfortably crisp collar of my new white shirt. 'I can't do this,' I thought to myself, poking at the button on my black jeans (which was threatening to burst at any moment). 'My stomach looks awful in these pants. They're going to judge me and realise I have no idea what I'm talking about. I'm not qualified enough for this.' This was me six years ago, getting ready to speak to a room full of people about anxiety — and there I was, ironically feeling very anxious. My inner critic was running rampant, picking at every possible perceived flaw, making me doubt my abilities and not-so-subtly trying to chip away at my confidence.

It's not you and it's not true

Does this little voice sound familiar to you? Meet the inner critic. A pesky-at-best, soul-destroying-at-worst, little voice in your head that takes great pleasure in pointing out to you all the ways in which you are 'not good enough'. Of course, everything it says is utter rubbish; repetitive thoughts and fears that serve only to shrink your confidence and hold you back. But there is something about this way of thinking that draws us in, somehow pulling us to listen to the inner critic's harsh comments and terrible advice.

Where does your inner critic come from?

You weren't born with this self-deprecating voice and habit. Your inner critic begins to develop in early childhood, and 'layers on' over the years, becoming more and more established. Initially, you learn this habit by taking on and internalising life experiences such as:

- Harsh judgements and comments directed at you from parents, caregivers and other important adults in your life.

- Criticisms from teachers, especially times when you felt ostracised, embarrassed or 'called out' in front of your peers.

- Taunts and snide remarks from bullies — if you think back to your school years, is there a comment from a peer that you have held on to, right to this day?

- Societal views and unhelpful narratives like 'it's weak to cry', 'success means a marriage, house and kids' and 'women should be beautiful and presentable while also holding down a job and raising children'.

A less direct, but equally damaging, way that your inner critic develops is through modelling. This happens when you take on the self-criticisms of someone important in your life. It's like developing an inner critic via osmosis! (I still remember that concept from high school biology class.) Here are some examples.

> Your mum always seemed to be on a diet. You remember her often commenting on her weight, what she was eating, how none of her clothes fit. While she may not have commented on your weight, you internalised the message that bodies are to be poked at, prodded and judged if they don't resemble something from the cover of a magazine. Via your mother's

actions and self-criticism, you learnt that certain foods were 'bad', that you needed to be harsh on yourself and that it was imperative you monitor your calorie intake.

Your dad was always stressed. He talked about finances in front of you, and you often overheard him berating himself for his performance at work. It seemed like nothing he did or had was good enough for him and he often worried out loud. From this you learnt that your worth was tied to your performance, and you learnt how to ruminate on your worries.

When we are modelled certain ways of relating to ourselves over and over again by someone important in our lives, or when we hear harsh and critical words directed at us from the people around us, we begin to internalise these messages as our own narrative. The words soon morph from sounding external to us, delivered in someone else's voice, to sounding like our own voice. The inner critic becomes indistinguishable from our own thoughts. It feels as though we are one and the same.

Katy sat behind her laptop on a Zoom coaching call with me. She picked at a loose thread on the hem of her blouse and described how she had never felt she was 'good enough'. Growing up, she had an overbearing mother who was quick to criticise her and seemed to clearly favour her older brother. Nothing Katy ever did seemed to measure up to this impossible set of standards. Even now, with a loving husband and two small children who adored her, she spent much of her day beating herself up and pointing out every small mistake. The week prior, I had tasked her with logging down her inner critic thoughts. Katy unfolded a piece of paper and read her statements out loud: 'Well, I dropped the milk so I thought, "I'm so useless." I thought, "I don't deserve my husband, I'm messing up my kids, I look fat and ugly today, I'm boring and frumpy . . ."' The list went on in this way.

It was clear to both of us that Katy had a strong inner critic that was steamrollering her confidence and hijacking her thoughts. This voice started out as the voice of her mother, but now, in her early thirties, Katy had well and truly internalised the voice as her own. Our work began in re-writing her story and serving her inner critic with an eviction notice.

How do you spot your inner critic?

Sometimes it is blatantly obvious when your thoughts are straight from the mouth of your inner critic. However, for many of us, we have spent years and years being harsh on ourselves and picking at our flaws. This has become a deeply ingrained behaviour and half the time we don't even realise we are doing it. Because of this, you may now be wondering how to disentangle and identify your inner critic thoughts from your own genuine views and beliefs.

Your mind is a busy hive of activity, thinking somewhere between 12,000 and 60,000 thoughts a day. There's no way you can check in and review all of these thoughts, so, how do you begin to spot your inner critic at work? Your emotions are the key. When you notice a feeling of anxiety, self-doubt, shame, insecurity, worthlessness or any other tricky emotion, stop. Pause. In this moment, ask yourself the following.

You might like to grab a journal and pen and jot down your answers to these questions, or log them on your phone's notepad in the moment. Chances are that your responses to these questions are actually your inner critic thoughts. This is your opportunity to interrupt the usual spiral of critical thoughts that lead you down the path of feeling awful about yourself. This is how we begin to 'call out' the inner critic.

Another way to identify your inner critic is to think of the areas in your life where you typically find yourself lacking in confidence and beating yourself up. Perhaps you notice you're always harsh on yourself when you do the final check in the mirror on your way out of the door. Or maybe you notice you always feel insecure in staff meetings at work, or that you're particularly cruel to yourself about not sticking to goals, like going for that walk at the end of the day. The next time you're in those moments, rather than continuing on autopilot, pause and check in with yourself. Ask:

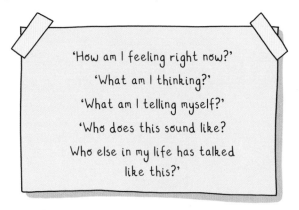

'How am I feeling right now?'
'What am I thinking?'
'What am I telling myself?'
'Who does this sound like?
Who else in my life has talked like this?'

Examine your answers to find out exactly what your inner critic is saying to you.

Your inner critic can be sneaky

Here is an element of your inner critic that you might not have known about: your inner critic actually plays a part in your unhealthy habits and self-sabotaging behaviours. Let me run this scenario by you . . .

You come home from work. It's been a long day, and your nerves overcame you in a meeting with your boss where you ended up jumbling your words and not getting across the point you wanted to. You're feeling deflated and defeated. You're thinking, 'Man, I tanked that meeting today. I'm so useless. I never get it right. Maybe I should just quit.'

Okay, that's an obvious inner critic thought, right? We can clearly see that. Now, watch it turn sneaky. You think, 'I should head out to the gym, sweat it out . . . but gosh, it's been such a draining day. Maybe I'll just sit on the couch, open a bottle of wine and some chocolate and scroll on my phone . . . just for five minutes.' So, you do. You have a glass of wine. You have a row of chocolate. You jump on Instagram and check out all the posts of people's glowing days, skin and holidays. You're feeling crap now. 'Today was so rough. I'll pour another glass, have another row, scroll a little longer . . . I deserve it,' you think. So, you do. You pour another glass. You eat another two rows of chocolate. You end up on some fitness page looking at a bunch of toned smiling women. You're feeling even worse now. 'I might as well just finish the bottle . . . There's only one row of chocolate left anyway, and I deserve it after that awful meeting with my boss . . .' So, you do.

Guess what happens now? The inner critic turns on you. You didn't even realise it was operating earlier, but it was, encouraging you to engage in unhealthy coping strategies under the guise of trying to make you feel better. And now?

Now it has all the ammo it needs to berate you for the very behaviours it just coaxed you into. Now you're thinking, 'I am so useless. I have zero self-restraint. I can't believe I drank the whole bottle; I'm going to turn into an alcoholic just like my mother. And there I go again, missing the gym for yet another night in a row to sit and eat chocolate. I might as well cancel my membership and give up. I can't stick to anything.'

The inner critic has come full circle, and now you're feeling worse than you did when you first got home. It has succeeded in convincing you to take part in unhealthy coping strategies by appearing sweet and offering comfort. But you know those strategies make you feel worse, and now the inner critic will use this as evidence to support the limiting beliefs that you are 'lazy' and 'useless'. What a vicious cycle. (More on limiting beliefs later, on pages 145–159.)

Is knowledge power?

It would be easy to feel a little depressed by all of this, maybe even a bit helpless and defeated. You might be thinking, 'Well, I've been this way for years. I'm conditioned to be this way thanks to my childhood, and I didn't even know my inner critic was so sneaky! It's hopeless.' Rather than finding this disempowering, however we can use this knowledge to our advantage; it is extremely empowering. Before we can make any change in life, we must first develop awareness — shining a spotlight on the issue so we can see and acknowledge it before we shift it. When you understand your inner critic, you have an opportunity to externalise this part of yourself that is no longer serving you.

Imagine your inner critic as the little 'devil on your shoulder',

> When you understand your inner critic, you have an opportunity to externalise this part of yourself that is no longer serving you.

or some other external pest that has been running amuck in your life. Now that you've met it, got to know how it came to be, and uncovered its sneaky tactics, you get to choose to relate to it in totally new ways, shedding yourself of its influence. You can call it out when you see it: 'Ahh . . . there goes my inner critic again! I see you!' You can choose to act against its bad advice: 'Thank you, inner critic — but actually, rather than opening the wine and chocolate, I'm going to go on a walk around the block and take some deep breaths.' You can let go of beliefs that came from your past that are no longer in your best interests: 'I know when I comment on my body like this that it comes from hearing my mother talk about herself like this. I can choose not to continue this pattern.'

'My inner critic does not serve my best interests. I have the power not to follow its bad advice or listen to its chatter'

Can you flip the script?

I am going to lead you through flipping the script on your inner critic. The first part of this can be rather confronting, so go easy on yourself.

1. Grab a pen and paper and write out the following headings: personality, career, looks, finances, friendships, relationships, family, strengths, weaknesses, body/physical features, education/skills. You are now going to write a description of how you see and speak about yourself to yourself in each of these parts of your life. This is just for you, so be honest about the words and language you use. Bullet points are okay.

2. Once you've finished your descriptions, go back through each one and highlight any harsh, critical or pejorative language. You are now identifying anything that sounds like your inner critic.

3. Pick a statement from your descriptions (or any other thought you find yourself getting caught up on that makes you feel like you're not enough in any way). Perhaps choose the statement you get stuck on the most to start with. For example, 'I'm so lazy', 'I have a flabby stomach', 'I'm terrible with finances', 'I'm a bad mother/wife/friend', 'I have a big nose', 'People don't like me'.

4. Switch this statement from an 'I statement' to a 'you statement' and write it out again, as follows.

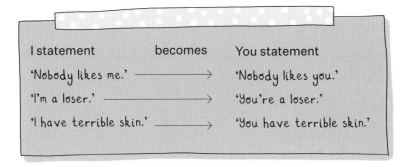

I statement	becomes	You statement
'Nobody likes me.'	⟶	'Nobody likes you.'
'I'm a loser.'	⟶	'You're a loser.'
'I have terrible skin.'	⟶	'You have terrible skin.'

5. Stand in front of a mirror or, ideally (and if you're feeling brave), grab someone you trust, tell them you are doing this exercise and say your 'you statement' out loud either to yourself in the mirror or directly to them.

See how it feels to do this — it was likely a confronting exercise, especially if you said your inner critic statement to someone else. It's hard to hear these things out loud. Turning your 'I statements' to 'you statements' helps to make them feel like a harsher, external and alien perspective.

*So — why not make friends with you
— and be a good friend at that.*

Would you speak like this to a friend? No. You wouldn't. And yet, you tolerate this language and way of speaking to yourself all the time. If you spoke to your friends the way your inner critic speaks to you, it wouldn't be long before the relationship broke down, leaving them feeling hurt and confused. Or, even worse, if they stuck around they would feel bullied as the hurtful words slowly chipped away at their confidence and self-worth. You don't get to break up with yourself! So — why not make friends with you — and be a good friend at that.

Can you change your inner critic?

We go about our lives believing what we believe and not questioning our thoughts. And that makes sense; not only would we be exhausted if we questioned everything, but it would feel like we were living life on shaky ground if we constantly evaluated our every belief. It's much easier just to steam ahead and follow the same habits and patterns we are used to (more on this later). Well, not anymore! You're here to challenge this inner critic business and, in doing so, you will begin to see a growing sense of confidence and self-love.

When you notice your inner critic at work, catch those thoughts and challenge them. Ask yourself:

- 'Is this thought really true?'

- 'Is this thought kind? Is it useful?'

- 'Who is served by thinking like this?'

- 'Where has this thought possibly come from? Where have I heard this before? Who has said this about me or about themselves in my life?'

- 'What evidence do I hold on to that I use to prove this thought to be "true"?'

- 'What is some evidence that this is NOT true?'

- 'What is another way to view this?'

- 'What if the opposite were true?'

- 'If my friend had this thought, what would I say to them?'

Use these questions to help you unpick and unpack, then re-write the inner critic statements as more balanced, compassionate and realistic thoughts. Here is a crucial thing to remember when developing a replacement thought:

We are not here to 'throw sugar on sh*t'

What this means is, we have to be able to believe the new thought. If you go to the extreme with your replacement thought, spurting off that things are all unicorns, glitter, love and light, then you won't believe it. If you change a thought from 'I'm such an anxious person' to 'I am full of confidence in everything I do', the chances are you won't buy it, because it isn't totally true. This is called 'cognitive dissonance', a term which refers to the mental discomfort that comes from having two conflicting beliefs. You simply can't accept the new belief because it is so far removed from your current reality. This is a key thing to remember when it comes to affirmations and creating new thoughts. We are aiming for replacement thoughts to be realistic, true, compassionate, helpful and balanced.

Here are some examples:

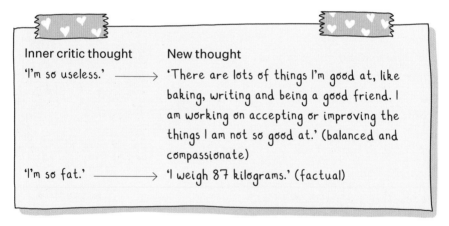

Inner critic thought	New thought
'I'm so useless.'	→ 'There are lots of things I'm good at, like baking, writing and being a good friend. I am working on accepting or improving the things I am not so good at.' (balanced and compassionate)
'I'm so fat.'	→ 'I weigh 87 kilograms.' (factual)

When you are really struggling to re-write an inner critic statement, you can use either gratitude or intention to replace it. For instance:

Inner critic thought	New thought
'I hate my stomach.' $\longrightarrow$	'I am grateful to my tummy for digesting my food/carrying my baby, etc.'
	or
	'I am working on speaking and using kinder words when thinking about my body.'

A tip on finding a balanced thought: write out your inner critic thought, then write out the complete opposite thought (one that is all unicorns and sparkles). This thought will likely cause you to screw up your nose in disbelief. Now, find the middle ground — write out a thought that feels neutral; something that doesn't bring up a big emotional reaction or pushback from you. That's the sweet spot.

EXERCISE

Now we need to re-write the 'self-narrative' you wrote in the exercise on page 24. Go back and look at all of the bits you highlighted (the harsh language of your inner critic) and, using your new skills in challenging your inner critic thoughts, re-write this description of yourself. Take out all of that pejorative language, replacing it with balanced statements, gratitude and fact. At the end, you should have a compassionate and realistic new self-description. Read and re-read this whenever you need it, and soak in this upgraded view of yourself.

A final note

Be patient and compassionate with yourself. It takes time to do this work. You may have spent years and years practising how to put yourself down, so it makes sense that it will take a bit of time and repetition to not only catch your inner critic at work, but to then change this pattern. And, more than that, it will likely also be met with resistance and feel uncomfortable.

We humans often dislike change. We don't like our beliefs being challenged, and it feels clunky and unnatural to create new habits. Speaking to yourself with kindness and compassion may feel foreign. Your inner critic may just push back, digging in its toes as it fights eagerly to stay in the driver's seat. So expect this to happen; it's normal. Sometimes, before we see the light, it can feel even darker. So, hang in there. This work is worth it.

Be patient and compassionate
with yourself.

Your Inner Worth

Just as true as it is that we all have an inner critic, so too do we have inner worth. The inner critic may have overshadowed this innate sense of truth and worthiness for some time, but trust that it is always there.

A simple way to begin to nurture and foster your self-worth is by creating your own 'inner coach'. If your inner critic is the devil on your shoulder, then your inner coach is the angel on the other shoulder.

EXERCISE

Bring to mind someone in your life who supports you and has your back; they could be living or no longer with us, real or imagined. When faced with your inner critic's chatter, turn to your inner coach. Ask yourself: 'What would this person say to me right now? What would they want me to know? What would they do to help me navigate this?' Perhaps also ask, 'What would I say to a friend?' Or, 'What would my best friend say to me?'

Another way to access your inner worth is to provide it space to come to the surface. It is especially useful to practise this in times of struggle or tricky emotions.

EXERCISE

Take a seat somewhere quiet and comfortable. Close your eyes and take five deep breaths into your belly. Repeat this phrase: 'I acknowledge my worth. I am enough.' Place your hand on your heart and ask yourself: 'What do I need right now?', 'What do I need to do to respect and honour myself?', 'What words do I need to hear?' Allow space to see what arises in response.

When you begin these practices, it's normal to feel like you aren't doing it right or it isn't working. Allow yourself some grace and keep practising. Following your inner coach creates vastly different outcomes than when you listen to your inner critic.

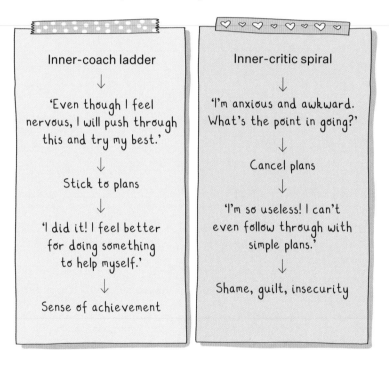

Inner-coach ladder

↓

'Even though I feel nervous, I will push through this and try my best.'

↓

Stick to plans

↓

'I did it! I feel better for doing something to help myself.'

↓

Sense of achievement

Inner-critic spiral

↓

'I'm anxious and awkward. What's the point in going?'

↓

Cancel plans

↓

'I'm so useless! I can't even follow through with simple plans.'

↓

Shame, guilt, insecurity

You'll further develop a sense of inner worth by working through the other chapters in this book, building upon your boundaries, re-writing your core beliefs and honouring your needs. Hang in there and keep reading.

Summary

- Your inner critic is not you, and it's not true.

- The inner critic develops by layering on years of unhelpful messaging you receive and modelling you observe. You can acknowledge this and choose to no longer act on the inner critic's bad advice.

- Your inner critic may be sneaky in its approach, coaxing you into unhealthy coping strategies then shaming you for the very behaviours it just encouraged. Keep an eye out for this.

- You have an inner worth that lives within you, just waiting to be accessed.

- Create an inner coach for yourself or ask yourself the question, 'Would I say this to a friend?' in order to tap into some self-compassion.

DECODE YOUR EMOTIONS

Your emotions are the language of your nervous system. In this chapter we'll explore the messages your emotions might be trying to send to you and how you can process them, rather than suppress them. Then you'll learn the role your nervous system plays in feelings of anxiety, anger, overwhelm, tension, racing thoughts and low motivation. In this chapter you'll learn some practical tools to assess, regulate and repair your nervous system.

Emotions

You are not alone if you find yourself actively rejecting certain emotions in your life. It's easy to lean into feelings of joy, happiness and love. But what about guilt, sadness, shame, grief and anxiety? They're uncomfortable; they don't feel great. So sometimes we don't accept or allow them. Instead, we find ourselves dismissing them, numbing them, avoiding them and pushing them down in our refusal to sit in their discomfort.

Pushing down tricky emotions is like trying to hold a beach ball underwater. It's not easy, and eventually the darn thing pops furiously back to the surface, sometimes in a completely different location. Sometimes it smacks someone in the face on its way up.

There are so many ways we try to suppress, hide from or mask our emotions. Some of us turn to shopping sprees at Kmart (not naming any names here . . . *ahem* myself). Some of us drink, binge-eat or smoke. We might drown ourselves in work, or bury our heads in the sand and block things out. Maybe we scroll mindlessly on our phones, or hide from solitude and silence by always being busy or around other people. Whatever it is that you do, it provides a temporary release. Long term . . . that beach ball is just waiting to pop up and bop you right in the nose.

'Emotions are not "good" or "bad", they are messages'

What if we changed the way we view emotions? What if we treated them as visitors showing up, temporarily, to deliver us a message? Consider that your emotions might be trying to nudge you towards meeting a need, or signalling something that requires your attention. Emotions are your nervous system's language of communication; your body's way of sending a message to your conscious mind. Sometimes emotions are a red flag to let you know that something in your life is off-kilter and you need to restore the balance. Other times they are sending you an invitation to simply take a look at something.

What are your emotions trying to tell you?

Sadness

Is saying: 'I'm feeling down and things are off-kilter. I'm trying to process something that doesn't feel right or okay.'

Needs: Care, support and space to be felt. Maybe time alone, maybe time to journal, maybe to connect with loved ones and be supported.

Ask myself: 'Who could I lean on for emotional support? How can I process this feeling? What can I do to look after myself right now?'

Loneliness

Is saying: 'I am feeling disconnected.'

Needs: To make connections with important people in my life. To lean on and embrace others.

Ask myself: 'Who can I reach out to for support? How can I foster connections?'

Anxiety

Is saying: 'I am feeling threatened and uncertain. My body is reacting in an effort to keep me safe.'

Needs: To allow this feeling without resistance, to remind myself I am safe, to take deep breaths and calm my nervous system and to step into discomfort without avoidance. To refocus in the present moment rather than 'time-travelling'.

Ask myself: 'What has triggered this feeling? What unhelpful thoughts or actions are fuelling it? What do I need to do to shift my focus? How can I remind myself of my resources and resilience?'

Guilt

Is saying: 'I have done something I don't feel good about that doesn't line up with my values' or 'I am people-pleasing and I need to step back and put my needs first'.

Needs: To put things right if I have made a mistake or hurt someone. Or, I need to forge ahead with my boundaries and prioritise my own needs for the sake of my long-term self-worth.

Ask myself: 'What can I do to make things right? How can I fix this problem? How can I learn from this in the future? What old limiting belief is being triggered with this guilt?' or 'Am I taking something too personally, or taking responsibility for something I shouldn't be?'

Anger

Is saying: 'A boundary has been crossed for me!' or maybe 'A deeper feeling has been triggered, and I'm feeling threatened by it.' Or maybe: 'I'm feeling overloaded and threatened.'

Needs: To pause and breathe. I need to take a timeout to process and release this feeling.

Ask myself: 'Are there any other emotions alongside or underneath my anger?' (Disappointment? Embarrassment? Hurt? Fear?) 'Has someone said or done something I don't like/am not comfortable with? Has a boundary been crossed? What can I do to safely express my anger? What can I do to calm myself? How can I effectively communicate this emotion? Am I emotionally overloaded?'

Insecurity

Is saying: 'I'm feeling out of my depth, unsupported, worried, judged or maybe afraid.'

Needs: Some support or reassurance and to remember all the things I have achieved and am good at. I need to remind myself that my worth is innate and not defined by external factors.

Ask myself: 'What do I need in this moment? How can I practise at this to gain confidence? What are the things I'm good at or that I know make me a worthy person?'

Resentment

Is saying: 'I am not speaking my truth in a relationship. My needs are not being met.'

Needs: To set boundaries, communicate my needs and find a place of compromise, respect and equality.

Ask myself: 'What value or need of mine is not being met? How can I address this feeling? What steps do I need to make to repair this? What do I need to communicate?'

Grief

Is saying: 'I have lost something or someone that is important to me and that is painful.'

Needs: To allow this emotion space. To reflect and remember. To nourish and care for myself.

Ask myself: 'How can I create some space for this process in my life? Who can I talk to for support? What kind of support do I need?'

Viewing emotions in this way, as messengers, helps to make some sense of them. When you do this, you pave the way to acceptance. Accepting your emotions doesn't mean you like them. No one enjoys feeling anxious, for example, but accepting that it's there — rather than pushing it away — actually begins the work of processing that emotion.

How can you process your emotions?

When you can name your feelings and allow emotions space, they can be processed. And, once processed, the emotion — like all visitors in life — passes through and takes its leave.

What you resist . . .   . . . persists

So the 'problem' isn't actually
the emotion; it is our reaction
to the emotion.

A crucial part of processing emotions is embracing the fact that none of the emotions you experience will last forever. No feeling is final. They come and they go. They change in their intensity. Some researchers say the actual physiological/biological lifespan of an emotion is only 90 seconds; that's how long it takes for it to pass through the body. So the 'problem' isn't actually the emotion; it is our reaction to the emotion. When we react, push back, judge and follow our emotions 'down the rabbit hole', they hang around for much longer. So the key, therefore, lies in changing our reaction to our emotions.

Here's the game-changer, and you may not like reading it: we have to learn to sit with discomfort. Rather than running from pain and avoiding suffering at all costs, we need to realise that going through these emotions is part of the human experience. Sitting with these emotions may be difficult, a rollercoaster even, but we are capable of it. We must ride it out, going with that emotional energy and trusting it will pass, rather than working against it.

Here are three tools to help you process your emotions.

The 'STOP' technique

Especially great to try when you notice feelings of anxiety or distress.

S	Stop	*What you are doing. Press pause.*
T	Take a Deep Breath	*Now take several more deep breaths into your belly. Breathe slowly.*
O	Observe	*Continue to breathe slowly and observe your thoughts. Tune in to your body and the physical sensations you are experiencing. Notice your present experience without judgement.*
P	Proceed	*Press play and proceed with something helpful and useful to you in this moment. Ask yourself: 'What do I need to do right now to look after myself?' Engage in self-care and be mindful about how you continue on in your day.*

The 'ALL' technique

 A **Acknowledge – Accept – Allow** Name how you are feeling or the thought you are having, e.g. 'This is anger' or 'I am noticing worries' or 'I'm being visited by sadness'. Sit with the feeling for as long as you need.

'I'm noticing sadness, and that's okay'

L **Link** Validate the feeling through linking it to something that helps you to understand or make sense of it.

'It makes sense that you (the feeling/thoughts) are here given that _____ (what you are going through)'. e.g. 'It makes sense that you are here given that I've had a lot of stress and loss lately'

L **Learn & Let it go** Ask what feeling is underneath the thought/Learn from the emotion: what message is it trying to send to you? What does it need?

Now, check in and ask yourself: 'Where do I feel this emotion in my body?' Place your hand on this area.

When you have given the emotion space and feel it might be ready to pass or that you are ready to pivot your focus, say 'I let this go now' or 'Thank you for your message, I allow myself to be free of this now'. Then you may like to physically 'brush off' the emotion with your hand from that area of your body, or even take a shower and imagine the emotion washing away.

'And that's okay' tool

When you notice an emotion, or even when you notice you are beating yourself up or being critical of something, try a little acceptance and compassion by ending your sentence with 'and that's okay'.

Your Nervous System

This section holds some great go-to techniques for coping when you are feeling overwhelmed by an emotion or you're dysregulated and needing some support to calm down.

Bear with me while I first explain, very simply, the autonomic nervous system and the threat responses (you'll find more information about anxiety, fear and your brain on pages 59–83). I'll keep this brief, and then we'll dive into some ways that you can support your nervous system and 'calm your farm'.

Your body hosts something called an autonomic nervous system; a complex system that regulates a whole heap of unconscious bodily processes like heartbeat, blood flow, digestion, breathing and more. The autonomic nervous system has two main branches: the sympathetic nervous system (SNS) and the parasympathetic nervous system (PNS).

You can think of the SNS as your stress response — it's the mode you switch into when you're feeling anxious or threatened. This response triggers the release of your stress hormones and gets things moving to keep you safe. The SNS is also all about movement and activation. In this state you might feel anxious, panicky, irritated, angry, rageful, stressed, and so on.

The PNS acts like a brake, slowing down the responses of the SNS. It is your rest, digest, restore and repair system. The sympathetic and parasympathetic nervous system work as a team, ramping you up and calming you down.

What is your vagus nerve?

Now let me introduce you to your vagus nerve — a cranial nerve that wanders throughout your body, beginning in your brain stem, travelling down your throat (larynx and pharynx) and branching out to connect with your lungs, heart, diaphragm, digestive system, the reproductive system and many other organs.

This vagus nerve is the main network of nerves in your PNS. It's like the body's 'chill pill', or your ability to bounce back from times of stress.

The vagus nerve has two branches of its own.

Ventral vagal: where you are calm and socially connected. A place you experience joy and playfulness. In this state you are able to be mindful and present, empathetic and resilient. This is what we think of when we think of the PNS; a place of peace and safety.

Dorsal vagal: this is your freeze response. This takes over when you are stressed and anxious for too long or your fear spikes too high — the dorsal vagal response will 'shut you down' (a bit like when your computer crashes), leaving you feeling flat, stuck, depressed, shamed, dissociated (disconnected from reality) or even immobilised. It's like your body's version of pressing control + alt + delete.

You can think of the whole system a bit like a car; your SNS is like putting your foot down on the accelerator, giving yourself some mobilisation, movement and thrusting into action. Your ventral vagal branch of the PNS is like pumping the brakes; you can apply a little or a lot in a controlled way in order to slow things down. Your dorsal vagal branch of the PNS is more like pulling on the handbrake/emergency brake; it's a little less regulated and controlled and helps to bring everything to a screeching halt, shutting down any movement.

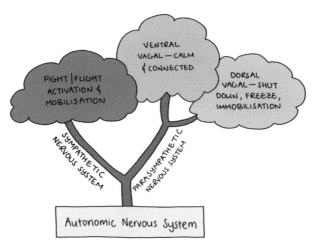

Something important to understand is that these threat responses happen quite outside of our conscious choosing. They are there to keep us safe, and if you have been through trauma or have been under a lot of stress and anxiety in your life then your nervous system can become more hypervigilant. You can reflexively fall into patterns of responding from a deregulated nervous system. Perhaps you notice you seem to habitually fall into people-pleasing, your posture slumping inwards as you feel flat or unmotivated. Maybe you have a tendency to snap easily, feeling irritated or angry as your body stiffens and braces around others. Or maybe you notice you carry your shoulders high, your jaw clenched, and you find it hard to be present as your mind races with worries. You might cycle between states, feeling anxious and on edge for weeks until your body fatigues and you fall into a state of depression (fluctuating between your SNS and dorsal vagal).

It is empowering to learn about these states and to become familiar with your own nervous system and reflexive ways of responding. When you are able to recognise your patterns and the somatic (body-based symptoms) and cognitive (thoughts and beliefs) experiences you notice in different states, then you can do the work in regulating and repairing your nervous system and learning new ways of responding.

Vagal tone

Now, no nervous system state is 'bad'. Your SNS is essential for survival — it is designed to switch on and get you out of a pickle, increasing your heart rate, diverting your blood away from your digestive system and into your limbs, flooding you with stress hormones and getting your body ready to zoom out of the path of sabre-toothed tigers. After this response, this system should really shut off. Your SNS is great at getting your body moving and providing you with the energy it needs to get things done, which is actually really useful in times of pressure and stress. And a bit of

SNS activation is great when combined with ventral vagal — the combination of movement and safety = play and dance!

Unfortunately, with the stressors of our modern-day lives, some of us spend prolonged periods of time in this fight-or-flight response. In fact, some of us live in such a sympathetic-dominant state that our vagus nerve actually loses tone and doesn't function as well as it should.

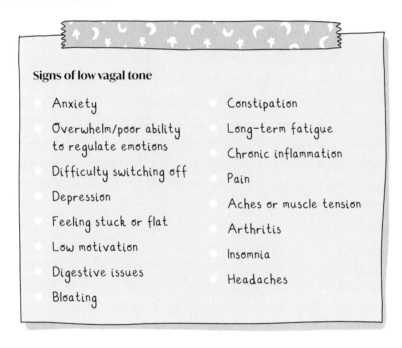

Signs of low vagal tone

- Anxiety
- Overwhelm/poor ability to regulate emotions
- Difficulty switching off
- Depression
- Feeling stuck or flat
- Low motivation
- Digestive issues
- Bloating
- Constipation
- Long-term fatigue
- Chronic inflammation
- Pain
- Aches or muscle tension
- Arthritis
- Insomnia
- Headaches

A cluster of these symptoms may show low vagal tone.

Nervous system states

Here are the states your nervous system is responsible for. (This fascinating explanation of humans comes from Dr Stephen Porges' Polyvagal Theory.)

Fight	Flight	Ventral Vagal (calm & connected)	Dorsal Vagal (Freeze)	Fawn
Sympathetic Nervous System		Parasympathetic Nervous System		Mixed state

Fight

Initiated by the SNS, this response springs your body into action, ready to fight away any threats. You might recognise this as anger, irritation, or a good old-fashioned adult tantrum!

Flight

Also initiated by the SNS, this response gears your body for action by urging you to run away or avoid anything you find threatening. You might recognise this when you feel like avoiding something that makes you anxious, or when you feel like leaving in the middle of an event that's causing you a lot of stress or fear. You might also recognise this if you find it hard to sit still, be in silence or focus on just one thing at a time. Flight response can show up as that 'go-go-go' energy, with overworking and overcommitting as you race through life.

Ventral Vagal (calm and connected)

A PNS state of calm, joy, social connection, empathy, and feeling relaxed and at ease. From this place you can access empathy, intimacy, compassion and reciprocity in relationships.

Dorsal Vagal (freeze)

The second branch of our PNS, this primitive threat response is a form of shutdown. This can occur if you've been stressed for too long or if you feel so afraid that your body shuts down. You might notice this if you feel depressed, stuck, flat, immobilised or unmotivated. It's common to drop into this more depressed state after a while if you're someone who experiences a lot of anxiety (after all, it's exhausting to be in an SNS state for too long). The freeze state can include some SNS activation also.

Fawn

A mixture of nervous system states, the fawn response is also called please and appease. You might notice this if you are a chronic people-pleaser, or someone who perhaps went through some trauma or emotional neglect during childhood where the only way to feel safe was to keep the people around you happy. You go into fawn response when you feel threatened and in order to cope you put on a brave face, try to keep everyone else around you happy and put aside your own needs and feelings. In this state you have activation of the SNS and freeze (dorsal vagal) response at the same time — it's like having your foot hard down on the accelerator of your car with the handbrake on at the same time. You also recruit your ventral vagal system in order to appear connected to people while using your smile and calm expression. (See pages 203–210 for more on people-pleasing.)

It is entirely normal to fluctuate between different states as your body responds to demand, stress and the needs of your environment.

There are also many mixed states of the nervous system, for instance:

- A mixture of SNS + ventral vagal gives us play, dance, joyful movement, healthy/fun competitive sport, as it is a mixture of mobilisation and safety.

- A mixture of dorsal vagal + ventral vagal gives us intimacy with its combination of immobilisation without fear.

How to improve vagal tone

The good news is that we can learn tools and techniques that activate our PNS, bringing us into our ventral vagal state and toning the vagus nerve. Just like working out a muscle at the gym, we can improve our vagal tone. What does that mean? It means more resilience, bouncing back from stress faster and being able to access your calm, along with a whole host of other health benefits. You can practise techniques that basically tell the vagus nerve to give feedback to the brain that 'all is well'!

Let me take you through a range of techniques that act to stimulate the vagus nerve, switch on the PNS and restore your calm. These are all wonderful ways to deal with those big, overwhelming emotions.

EXERCISE

This is important and the perfect place to start. Name your emotions and identify the nervous system state you are in. If you can state aloud the emotion you are feeling, this helps calm the emotional centre of your brain. And if you can recognise when you are in a fight-or-flight or freeze response you can take action. Try this check-in to help you do this:

On a scale of 1-10, how is my body feeling?

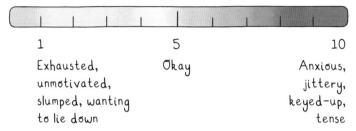

1	5	10
Exhausted, unmotivated, slumped, wanting to lie down	Okay	Anxious, jittery, keyed-up, tense

If you are closer to a 1, you need to 'up-regulate' your nervous system. Try pushing your feet into the floor, pushing against a wall, stretching, going for a walk, and so on. If you are closer to a 10, you need to 'down-regulate' your nervous system. Try relaxing your muscles, softening your feet into the floor, gentle stretching, deep belly breaths with longer exhales, and so on.

On a scale of 1-10, how are my thoughts?

1	5	10
Spacey	Okay	Racing, incoherent, ruminating

If you are closer to a 1, you need to get grounded. Do this by focusing on a sense (try smelling an essential oil like peppermint or lemon), running cold or warm water on your hands, sucking on a candy that is sour or has a strong flavour, tuning in to your breath, engaging in a conversation with someone or doing some journalling. If you are closer to a 10, calm your thoughts with mindfulness — focus on noticing colours or textures in the room, take deep belly breaths, focus on your sense of smell (try smelling an essential oil like ylang ylang or lavender), do a brain-dump or find a way to distract yourself.

How to restore your calm

- Try humming, chanting or singing . . . these all send vibrations down your vocal cords (which the vagus nerve runs along), thus stimulating the nerve and activating a sense of calm. So, you have my (and science's) full permission to 'get your hum on'!

- Plunge your face into a bowl of cold water up to your temples for 30–60 seconds. This stimulates something called a 'dive reflex', which instantly slows down your heart rate to conserve oxygen. This is an incredible technique for rapidly easing feelings of anxiety, stress or panic and for elevating your mood. You can also hold a good old bag of ice or frozen peas against your chest, the back of your neck or your face from your hairline to your lips.

- Meditate. Try a guided version if you're just getting started and want some help.

- Expose yourself to cold. Try a cold shower — or a 30-second cold blast at the end of your shower should do it!

- Have a massage. There are spots in your ears and down your neck you can massage, but have a good google of tutorials so you don't do it wrong!

- Gargle water loudly — maybe in the shower, before your cold blast?! The sensation activates the vagus nerve in your neck.

- Do some belly breathing, or any breathing technique that speaks to you. I cannot stress enough the power of your breath. When you're stressed, anxious, panicking or overwhelmed, you begin to breathe faster, higher up into the chest. Those under chronic stress or anxiety often have a high breathing rate per minute (ideally you want your breathing rate to be between twelve  and sixteen breaths per minute, and not over twenty). When you over-breathe, you throw out the balance of carbon dioxide and oxygen in your system and this causes a whole host of symptoms, from anxiety to insomnia, headaches and fatigue to lightheadedness and the inability to think clearly. A high breathing rate is a sign you're in a sympathetic nervous system dominant state. So try slowing those breaths right down — aim for six breaths per minute or just focus on breathing fully into your diaphragm.

- Practise mindfulness — notice emotions, thoughts and physical sensations without judgement. Accepting and allowing. Naming and acknowledging, with curiosity.

- Do sun salutations/yoga.

- Cross your arms over your chest, place your hands on your shoulders and alternately tap your hands in a slow, calming rhythm while breathing deeply into your belly.

There are many other methods you can try, so research further if this floats your boat! (I have courses on soothing your nervous system at journeytowellness.online)

I suggest picking a couple of the tools from above and trying them as a daily practice for two to four weeks. See how you feel, and what changes in or for you. Remember, practice makes progress.

In learning to repair and regulate the nervous system, you can un-learn old patterns or reflexive responses that no longer serve you. You can strengthen your resilience and ability to find a place of safety and calm in your own body. I've found it helps us to build self-compassion when we learn that our body is responding in these ways to keep us safe, and that maybe it has just got a little over-sensitive or stuck in its ways. It also teaches us to tune in and listen to our bodies, reading our somatic symptoms and learning to respond in ways that restore balance.

Well done for wading through all the info in this chapter! While it can feel a little 'heavy', it can also be life-changing to understand your nervous system.

So, there you have it — you really can 'calm your farm'!

Summary

- Emotions are your body and nervous system communicating with you.

- Treat your emotions as visitors or messengers — get curious about what they might be trying to tell you.

- It's okay to take a break from your feelings sometimes, but don't fall into the trap of suppressing, masking or hiding from your emotions as a default. Remember: what you resist persists.

- Name your emotions. Notice them in your body. Allow them to be there. This helps to process them.

- Your nervous system has a range of automatic threat responses and states: fight, flight, freeze and fawn. Each of your nervous system states is there to serve, protect and guide you — however, we can become stuck in reflexive patterns of responding that are no longer helpful for us.

- You can build your resilience and capacity by tuning in to your nervous system and finding ways to soothe and regulate yourself.

STEP OUT OF THE OF THE WORRY TRAP

There are so many ways you might be
stuck in the tiresome trap of worrying —
perhaps focusing on things outside of
your control, burrowing into your comfort
zone or succumbing to avoidance.
In this chapter we'll explore why it is
you worry and how to break free from
the many ways worry sucks you in.

Worry

Most of us have experienced times of worry in our lives. Some of us worry all the time. One thing we can probably agree on is that worry isn't fun. It doesn't feel good. So, why do we do it?! Well, the answer is a complex mixture of genetics, modelling, environment, habits, core beliefs . . . the list goes on. One explanation is that worry, in part, is a genetic and evolutionary mechanism.

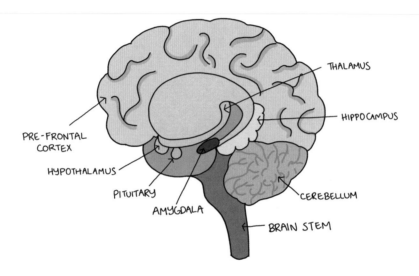

Let me explain anxiety and your brain. Back in the caveman days, it was crucial that you were always on the lookout for things that might eat you. Scanning your environment for danger was the only way you had a chance of survival. A structure in your brain called the amygdala is partly responsible for this role — scanning and alerting, always on the lookout.

Imagine caveman-you was out looking for berries when you

heard a rustle in the bushes, then a low growl, and you turned to see the tail of a sabre-toothed tiger approaching through the long grass. This triggered the amygdala's alarm system and it kicked your body into a sympathetic nervous system state, sending an instant signal down your brain stem to your adrenal glands, and promptly flooding your system with stress hormones like cortisol and adrenalin. There was no time to stop and think — only time to sound the alarm and spring into action to high-tail it out of there!

This threat response is called the fight-or-flight response, and it's designed to keep you safe. In this state of stress you experience all kinds of physical symptoms, like a racing heart, fast breathing, sweating, dizziness, a nervous tummy . . . all due to stress hormones and a redirection of blood flow. This is your body preparing to run or fight for your life.

Going forward, caveman-you would hypervigilantly look out for these same threats again. Any time you heard a rustle in the bushes, your body would instantly respond; it didn't matter if it was just a bird — your amygdala had strongly encoded the memory of fear and threat. Both the amygdala and the thinking part of your brain (pre-frontal cortex) like to be on the lookout for anything that might go wrong, and thus began the evolutionary task of worrying.

When we fast-forward to today, worrying has become far more complex. Your survival brain doesn't care if the threat is real or only perceived, or even imagined. Gone are the sabre-toothed tigers and real life-threatening situations on a daily basis. But there are work deadlines, never-ending bills, endless choices to be made, car breakdowns, concerns for your health . . . All of these modern-day sabre-toothed tigers have us up at night ruminating or stuck in a spiral of stress and overwhelm.

No amount of worrying or ruminating about an issue will solve it or stop it.

Many of us actually fall into the trap of worrying habitually. You might think (possibly unconsciously) that if you worry about something enough you can somehow control it, as if imagining all the worst-case scenarios or going over and over something will actually prevent the thing from happening or prepare you somehow. The truth is, we just aren't that powerful! No amount of worrying or ruminating about an issue will solve it or stop it. (Problem-solving and worrying are two different things!)

Imagine you have a 'worry part': a little monster in your brain that loves to worry. You might like to name your worry part (I personally call my worry part Patricia); think of someone who annoys you or imagine a silly character, maybe with little horns or a top hat and a monocle for good measure. This worry part has

decided that the best possible way to keep you safe is to alert you to every possible concern coming up. Ideally, if it had its way, it would like you to think about those things at all times, maybe even just stay home curled in a ball on the couch, never straying from your comfort zone.

The worry part has an insatiable appetite — no amount of reassurance you give to it will satisfy its hunger for worry. Every time you engage with it, it's like you are feeding it a little pellet, keeping its appetite and motivation for pestering you alive.

Picture this scenario: you have a function coming up where your workplace and a few others will be coming together at seven o'clock on Friday evening. You're not sure who is going from your work and you don't know anyone from the other businesses. Let's now imagine the dialogue between your worry part and you as you try to calm your nerves and silence your worry . . .

Worry Part: *Oh my gosh, what if we don't know anyone there?!*

You: *I'm sure at least a few people from work will be going.*

Worry Part: *But WHO?! Who from work? Because we don't like Susan, and Neil spits when he talks so we don't want to be stuck with him . . . unless we can bring an umbrella!*

You: *It's fine, at least there will be someone I know to talk to.*

Worry Part: **gasp* But what if we have to do an ice-breaker exercise?! What if we have to mingle with people from the other businesses?!*

You: *Oh gosh . . . yes, I hate talking to people I don't know . . . maybe I can go on the Facebook event and see who has RSVP'd.*

Worry Part: *What kind of event is it, though?! It's at 7 p.m. on a Friday night . . . you should wear a cocktail dress.*

You: *That's fine — it won't matter what I wear.*

Worry Part: *Oh, but what if everyone comes from work in business attire?! You'll look like an idiot in a dress! You should cancel!*

You: *I'll message some colleagues to see if they are going and what they are wearing.*

What do you notice about the worry part? You might notice that it does an awful lot of catastrophising. You might also notice it starts a lot of sentences with 'What if . . . ?' That 'What if . . . ?' is your worry part's favourite question. It adores planting seeds of doubt, with the ultimate goal to:

- Get you to think through all of the possible worst-case scenarios (bless its misguided wee heart — it is trying to keep you safe, after all);

- Get you to avoid the situation that is alarming it;

- Keep you engaged in a dialogue, trying to pacify it and soothe the anxiety that comes with it.

You might also notice that the worry part entices you into behaviours to try to calm it. Each time you answer back, trying to placate it with reassurance and double-checking, you feed it a pellet. Your worry part wants three things: certainty, comfort and control (I call these the three Cs, and they are what anxiety is always seeking to find). These three things are lovely, but we can't always have them.

Certainty: We can't always know for sure the outcome or how something is going to be.

Comfort: We don't grow when we stay in our comfort zone; there are going to be times in life that are hard and uncomfortable.

Control: We can't control the outcome of all things in life, we can't control a lot of things!

In our example above, the worry part entices some of the three C behaviours: checking the Facebook event and scrolling through the invite list, and messaging colleagues to see what they are wearing. It's also trying to get you to cancel on the event entirely. Here is what is going on with this dialogue: you are playing a game of tug of war with worry. Every time you engage in this conversation with worry, you play its game. It's always up to the same old tricks. But we fall into the trap of thinking maybe it will go away if we can just keep trying to placate it.

The true way out of the worry trap is to DROP THE ROPE . . . stop feeding Patricia pellets!

When you let go, stop engaging in the worry game and drop the rope, you stop adding fuel to the fire. I like to say, 'Oh hi there, Patricia . . . no tug of war for me today, thanks!' before pivoting my attention. And here's what you can pivot your attention to: things you can control. Meet me on the next page to explore this further.

Control

When it comes to managing worry, lifting your self-worth and boosting your mood, an empowering step forward is to shift your focus to things that are within your circle of control. Consider the control circles:

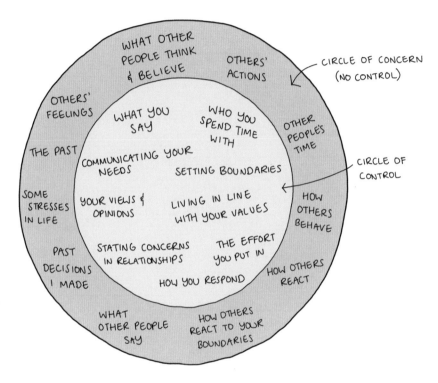

This illustration gives you an example from a broad sense about some of the things that are inside your control versus what isn't.

You can create your own control circle. Try it for specific issues you are facing. Let me show you how by introducing Krista. Krista had been with her partner Bryce for five years, and she came along to see me to talk about her frustration with her relationship and her struggles with feeling stressed and stuck. Krista was in a pattern of focusing on the things in her life that were outside of her control (in her circle of concern), and as a result she was feeling hopeless and helpless to create changes. Krista's focus looked like this:

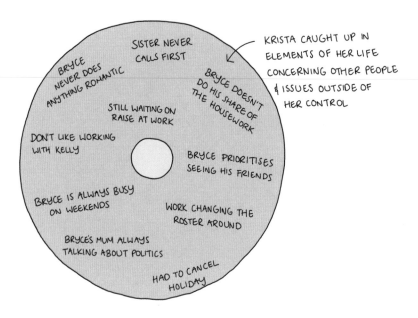

You can see that Krista was feeling weighed down by the behaviours of other people in her life, fixating on these things and feeling frustrated and overwhelmed as to why she was seeing no changes. Krista's mission was to flip the focus, bringing her attention back to her power and back to her own circle of control. This is what that looked like for Krista:

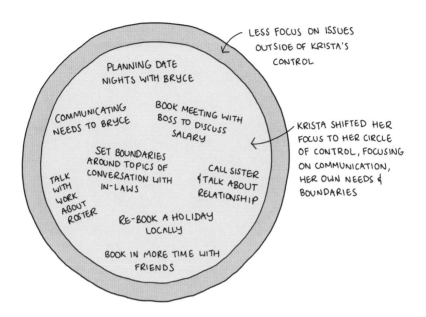

LESS FOCUS ON ISSUES OUTSIDE OF KRISTA'S CONTROL

PLANNING DATE NIGHTS WITH BRYCE

COMMUNICATING NEEDS TO BRYCE

BOOK MEETING WITH BOSS TO DISCUSS SALARY

SET BOUNDARIES AROUND TOPICS OF CONVERSATION WITH IN-LAWS

TALK WITH WORK ABOUT ROSTER

CALL SISTER & TALK ABOUT RELATIONSHIP

RE-BOOK A HOLIDAY LOCALLY

BOOK IN MORE TIME WITH FRIENDS

KRISTA SHIFTED HER FOCUS TO HER CIRCLE OF CONTROL, FOCUSING ON COMMUNICATION, HER OWN NEEDS & BOUNDARIES

For Krista, changing her focus and taking back her power didn't guarantee that life would be peachy. She couldn't change the people in her life — how they acted, what they believed and so on. But she could change the way she responded to them.

The same applies to you. You can shift your focus from external to internal. Like Krista, this focus shift won't change the people in your life (but it may just influence them and your relationship with them), and it won't change the stressful things taking place in the world — the weather, bills, the past . . . So while you can't do a lot about things outside of your control, you can clearly state your needs and expectations in relationships. You can set consequences for people who do not respect your boundaries. You can change the way you respond to your own thoughts. You can change the way you spend your time and energy. And doesn't that feel like a far more productive and empowering place to come from in your approach to life?

How do you address your worries?

When I have a worry or a concern pop up in my life, I ask myself a series of questions. They work like a flow chart (pictured opposite).

My flow chart breaks problems down into three categories, as below.

1. In your circle of control

Problems that fit here can be actively worked on — there are solutions and options for you to take. This doesn't make it easy; there may still be pain or discomfort. However, spending your energy and focus here is a more empowering place to be. Here you can make clear plans, take actionable steps, be clear that this is your own responsibility and make changes. For example:

- 'I'm unhappy in my job. I can: take steps to address issues with my boss, ask for a transfer to a new position, request a change in work hours/days, quit, stick it out for a bit while I look for a new job, etc.'

- 'My new partner has said some nasty things to me. I can: clearly state my limits to my partner, set consequences, set clear and firm boundaries, discuss my feelings and needs with my partner, take a break from the relationship, leave the relationship, etc.'

2. In your circle of influence

Many of the things that you cannot control can be shifted into this

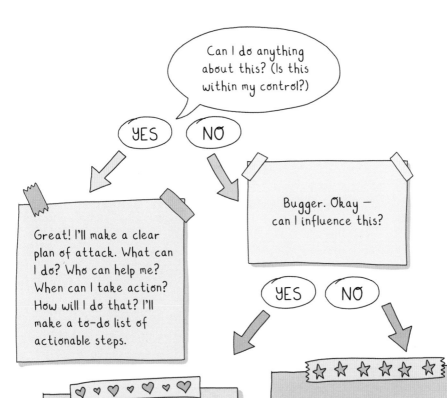

Can I do anything about this? (Is this within my control?)

YES

NO

Great! I'll make a clear plan of attack. What can I do? Who can help me? When can I take action? How will I do that? I'll make a to-do list of actionable steps.

Bugger. Okay — can I influence this?

YES

NO

I can take some small actions to either change the outcome or change my response to it. Do I need to influence how I feel about this worry by keeping a very close eye on my unhelpful thinking styles? If this problem is a person, can I influence it by speaking with this person?

Right, okay — this issue is therefore outside of my control. Now, what do I need to do to process the worry around this? How can I support my emotional reaction to this issue, given I cannot change it? I need to support my nervous system through this worry and switch my focus to other things that are within my control. How can I let this go? What do I need to sit with the discomfort of this right now?

Some things are just not within
your ability to control or change.

category in one way or another. You can influence problems in your
life by bringing your attention and focus back to what you can do.
You might influence an issue simply by changing the behaviours
you engage in or the way you are responding to your thoughts. For
example:

- 'I have a bad relationship with my mother-in-law. While I can't
  change my mother-in-law, I can: be mindful of how much time
  I spend with her, take responsibility for my contribution in the
  relationship, be respectful and amicable in the way I speak to her,
  go to therapy to manage the conflicting emotions I have around
  this, journal about my feelings as a healthy way to vent, etc.'

- 'I have been diagnosed with a health issue. While I can't
  change the diagnosis, I can: take steps in areas of my life to
  improve my overall health, exercise within my limits to reduce
  stress, eat a diet that supports this new issue, seek counselling
  for support, set new boundaries to support my energy, take
  care of my stress levels, get adequate sleep, etc.'

3. In your circle of concern

Some things are just not within your ability to control or change. If
you spend too much time and energy on these things, you will be
left feeling frustrated, drained and hopeless. While not always easy,
you need to find ways to release the focus and reduce the time and
energy you give to things that fall in this category. For example:

- 'My step-father has conflicting political views to me. I can't change his opinion and beliefs. I will bring this into my influence/ control by setting clear boundaries about what I will and won't discuss, or where is appropriate to discuss things and where isn't (for instance, not at the dinner table). Or I will find a way to let it go; I can't change his views. His views do not invalidate my own. I will allow both of us to have our own beliefs.'

- 'I planned a picnic with my family and now it's raining. I can't change the weather. This event is cancelled and there is nothing I can do. I will bring this into my influence/control by rescheduling the event and planning a wet-weather activity for the day, like going to the movies.'

You might be thinking, 'Well, that's all well and good, but how do I let go of things that are outside of my control?!' To let things go, we can take a similar approach to what we explored on pages 60–66 about the worry part, or try the ideas ahead about taming your thoughts. This is all about mindfully observing something for what it is, without trying to change it or fight against it. When you fixate on things you can't change, it's like pouring your energy into a bucket riddled with holes. You can't do anything about the fact that everything is going to leak out all over the place, and ultimately you are completely wasting your time.

Changing the path you're on and letting go of things that are outside of your control may not feel natural or easy. And that's okay.

It's hard to let go of things, though, isn't it? Here is a funny example:

Pick up an object near you — maybe a pen, or something similar — and hold it in your hand. Stare at it and tell yourself over and over for the next 30 seconds: 'Do NOT let this go. Do NOT drop it. Hold on. DON'T let go,' and so on. After 30 seconds, pause and then . . . drop it. Tell yourself to let it go and drop it. Pause your reading here and do this exercise. I'll wait.

What happened? You may have observed an interesting thing occurring here. Did you pause? Did you find it just a little tricky to uncurl your fingers at first? Maybe you didn't want to let go, or maybe you just found yourself questioning the activity or pausing a little longer before releasing.

This happened after just 30 seconds of you telling yourself to hold on to the object. Imagine what it is like for your brain to let go of a worry, a concern, a relationship, a job, a fixation, when you have been holding on to that thing for much longer.

Changing the path you're on and letting go of things that are outside of your control may not feel natural or easy. And that's okay. It doesn't have to. What you do need to do is commit to the act and the intention of letting go when you know it is out of your control and you know it doesn't serve you.

Here are a few symbolic rituals I like to do when I am trying to let go of worries or unhelpful thinking patterns or beliefs about myself.

Wash it all away

Have a shower, and imagine that the water running off you is stripping away your worries and the things you are holding on to that are outside of your control. Visualise these things running down the drain. Maybe repeat the mantra, 'I let this go now. This is washing away.'

Journal it

Grab your pen and paper and dump it all down. Get all the things that are out of your control written out in a stream of consciousness purge. Then . . .

Trap it

Take the paper and trap those things you've written in a jar with a lid or . . .

Burn it (safely)

Set fire to the paper and watch the worries go up in smoke. Repeat the mantra, 'I let you go now. I release you.'

Your Comfort Zone

Oh, comfort zone . . . you delightful thing, you . . . why must we ever part ways? When I think of my comfort zone, I picture a cosy nook in my house, fluffy socks, Netflix, a hot water bottle, a cup of tea and a candle going. And do you know what? There is nothing wrong with that at all.

It is perfectly okay to live a portion of your life in your comfort zone. Everyone will have their own version of a comfort zone, the common denominators being that it feels easy, comfortable, routine, predictable, non-threatening and we can exist in that space without much thought — running on autopilot.

And we absolutely do need this in our life. If we were always pushing the envelope, challenging ourselves and stepping into the unknown, it might feel rather overwhelming for our nervous systems. So, while it is fine to operate from your comfort zone, you certainly don't want to be there at all times. Why, you ask? Because your comfort zone is not where growth happens.

Stepping out of your comfort zone means the creation of new neural pathways, and trying new things. It means the formation of new habits and the breaking of old habits, it means embracing your fears head-on and expanding your world. And let's be clear: in order to do something new, to be courageous and bold, you do

not have to be fear-free. This is not courage; courage is feeling the fear and stepping into that fear. Leaning in. Don't wait until you feel confident before you try something new; that's not how you grow. Do the new thing — even if you have to do a nervous wee ten times before you do it, and even if you do it with a sweat moustache and a shaking voice!

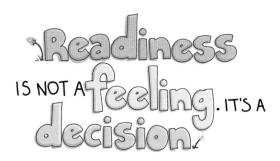

Your comfort zone can even be a bad place for you. If you are someone who is used to toxic relationships, suppressing your needs, overworking, mindless scrolling, suppressing your emotions — any number of unhelpful behaviours — these may actually feel comforting to you. Comforting because they are routine and familiar to your brain. In times like this, you must understand that your comfort zone is not safe, but familiar. And it isn't working for you in your best interests.

Stepping out of your comfort zone may well activate your threat response; new things often do because they feel unfamiliar and scary. When you feel that whoosh of fear or those racing thoughts of worry, there is a cycle that threatens to activate: the avoidance cycle. When we avoid things because of fear, this is our flight response in action (you'll find all the info on these responses on pages 45–57). Avoidance is the ultimate flight response — not showing up in the first place saves all that running, right? But avoidance is a vicious cycle that begins to shrink our worlds and possibilities. It goes a little something like this.

THE 'THING'

THAT YOU'RE AFRAID OF
(an event, person, situation, feeling etc)

INCREASED THREAT RESPONSE, HYPERVIGILENCE & NEGATIVE ASSOCIATION WITH SIMILAR 'THINGS'

Worries, thoughts, fears, mind reading & predictions about the 'thing'

PHYSICAL ANXIETY

SHORT TERM = RELIEF
LONG TERM = CONFIRMS FEAR OF THE 'THING', CEMENTS ANXIETY, REINFORCES ESCAPE & AVOIDANCE BEHAVIOURS

SYMPTOMS

LEAVE, ESCAPE OR AVOID THE 'THING'

EXIT

INCREASED FOCUS ON SELF, THREAT, THOUGHTS, ANXIETY & 'MAGNIFICATION' OF FEAR OF THE 'THING'

The act of avoidance actually confirms and cements our fears.

This explains why we fall into patterns of avoiding things, right? It feels good! You avoid 'the thing' and you feel instantly better, the weight is lifted, you feel relieved. This reinforces the avoidance. BUT, the long-term consequence of this avoidance is much greater than we might realise. The act of avoidance actually confirms and cements our fears. Our brains say, 'Oh gosh, I remember this thing. I had to avoid it last time . . . so it must be a threat!' Your avoidance of this 'one thing' begins to spread. Your brain begins to recognise other things that look a little bit like the threat and freak out about all of them.

As this pattern of avoidance continues, our world grows smaller and smaller. Our comfort zones close in around us. And it's not just places or things we avoid; we avoid emotions, we try to avoid certain thoughts, we avoid putting ourselves out there and being authentic, we stop trying. I don't want this for you. And I'm sure you don't want it for yourself.

All this being said, how do we break the avoidance cycle? The answer is simple (but not easy): avoid avoidance! You have got to actively step in and step out. Do the things that you have been avoiding (and yes, it's okay if you scale up to them, easing your way in). Step out of your comfort zone and into your growth zone deliberately, with the intention that you want your world to be expansive.

You probably have some specific things that are coming to mind that you have been avoiding. These are the things you need to

Step out of your comfort zone and into your growth zone deliberately, with the intention that you want your world to be expansive.

start doing. But if you feel like you need a confidence booster first, you can do this by picking some activities from the list below to experiment with. These are hopefully smaller and more manageable challenges to get your metaphorical ball rolling! All of these exercises are designed to do at least one of the following:

- Get you to step out of your comfort zone and into your growth zone.
- Help you to speak your mind, find your voice and state your needs.
- Challenge your anxiety.
- Push back against perfectionism and procrastination.

- Spark up a conversation with someone you haven't spoken to before, or someone you don't know well. This could be a colleague at work, or someone at the bus stop.

- Make a phone call instead of texting or emailing.

- Go for a walk on a route you haven't taken before.

- Navigate somewhere without using your GPS.

- Order a coffee (or anything really) at a cafe, then when the waitstaff tell you the price, change your order to something else.

- Send food back if it isn't what you ordered or it isn't quite right.

- Send an email without spell-checking.

- Set a boundary. Start small, but start somewhere. How about saying no to overtime at work this week, and yes to taking your lunch breaks on time?

I urge you to try out some (or all) of the things on this list, or to write your own list. I know it doesn't feel easy, but if it did we'd be missing the whole point, right? You can do hard things.

Now, before you slam this book down in a fit of defiance because you just don't want to step out of your comfort zone — especially if that means being in a place of panic or fear — I want you to understand this: there is actually a third zone, which lies outside of your growth zone, called the panic zone. And this is not where I am asking you to go. It is one thing to push yourself, to stretch your abilities and lean into some discomfort and unease for the sake of growth. It is entirely another to be in a place full of fear, feeling as though your alarm bells are ringing and your body has gone into a threat response. Being in a place of extreme panic is not the best way to learn something new or to experience success.

To overcome avoidance and to step into the best version of yourself, you want to feel that you are challenging yourself, maybe experiencing some discomfort or manageable levels of fear AND then having experiences of success in this place. When this happens, your comfort zone will begin to expand. More and more things will begin to feel natural to you, things you might never have thought you could achieve. Sitting with emotions, allowing yourself to prioritise your own needs, setting boundaries — all of this will become accessible to you.

> By building trust in yourself through action, you will build evidence that you are capable and you will be more willing to step into growth and change.

And as your comfort zone expands, things that were once in your panic zone will be swallowed up by your growth zone. By building trust in yourself through action, you will build evidence that you are capable and you will be more willing to step into growth and change.

Summary

- Worry is a normal, evolutionary function. However, some of us get caught up in the worry trap, always listening to our worry parts.

- Drop the rope on your worry — don't engage in a tug of war.

- As much as you can, focus on things that are within your circle of control and influence.

- It's okay to spend time in your comfort zone, but you will need to step out into your growth zone in order to expand, grow and change.

- Readiness is not a feeling; it is a decision. Make the conscious choice to lean into discomfort and expand your world.

- Avoidance fuels anxiety, makes you hypervigilant and shrinks your world.

- Try purposefully doing things that you are avoiding or that are outside of your comfort zone in order to build tolerance for discomfort and provide yourself with evidence that you are capable.

BREAK FREE FROM SELF-SABOTAGE

Self-sabotage shows up in many (sometimes sneaky) ways. Here we'll explore the ways that distractions, unhealthy coping strategies, perfectionism and procrastination are holding you back from being your best self. And of course, we'll do more than just explore them! You're going to learn some tools and strategies to rise above self-sabotage and build trust in yourself.

Coping Strategies & Distractions

When it comes to unhealthy coping strategies and unhelpful distractions, there are many reasons we engage in them, even though we know they aren't good for us or serving our best interests. Here are some of those reasons.

- These are our 'default pathways'. It's just plain easy for our brains to choose these behaviours because they are habitual. Our brain doesn't have to think much; it gets to go on autopilot and it quite likes that.

- Our brains prefer 'familiar discomforts' to unfamiliar ones. Binge-scrolling on social media is a familiar discomfort because we feel crappy after doing it, but at the time it is known to us so feels comfortable to our brains. The brain will choose things that feel familiar — even if they are unhealthy or painful — because the familiar is less threatening and requires less effort.

- Our brains seek instant gratification. Often we choose things that give us an instant hit of dopamine, a sense of reward or comfort right now. Cue the social media scrolling again!

- We prioritise short-term comfort and long-term pain over short-term pain and long-term growth. Feel free to read that point again. Eating a whole block of chocolate to suppress our emotions feels good right now, even though it hurts us in the long term (poor nutrition, body image impact, takes us away from our goals of a healthy body, etc.). The alternative is to go through the pain of not eating the chocolate now and dealing with your emotions in the short term, and then long-term building your sense of self-trust and self-worth. Obviously the latter is the outcome we want, but because there is no instant gratification or result, we don't do it. (P.S. Don't get me wrong here — I love chocolate! I just needed an example. Quite frankly, sometimes the exact thing you need is to eat it and drop the self-judgement!)

So, next time you are facing the choice 'Do I engage in this unhealthy behaviour/distraction or not?', ask yourself:

- 'Is this good for me?'
- 'Does this move me towards my goals or away from my goals?'
- 'Is this behaviour actually me trying to numb, distract or suppress an emotion?'
- 'Am I using this as a tool to cope with (or avoid coping with) my feelings?'
- 'Is this in my best interests?'
- 'Is this what I want?'
- 'Would future-me be happy about this decision?'

If you do choose to engage in the distraction behaviour — e.g. you decide you do want to scroll on social media or binge out on Netflix — do so intentionally, consciously, mindfully and in moderation. NOT as a substitute for sitting with and feeling and dealing with your emotions. This might look like this.

> *'Okay, I choose to watch back-to-back TV programmes right now because it's what I want and I need the chill time.*

However, after this I will set aside some time to journal on the feelings I am experiencing right now and do some meditation to sit with them and allow them space.'

Or

'I choose to eat some sugary foods right now, but rather than mindlessly eating a cake of chocolate when I'm sad, I will eat some chocolate slowly, mindfully, intentionally and WITHOUT layering on the guilt afterwards. It is okay for me to eat chocolate if that is what my body wants.'

Okay, so on to the octopus exercise . . . stick with me here; I promise the use of this sea creature will make sense! Draw the following octopus template on a bit of paper at home, including the rocks and guide lines.

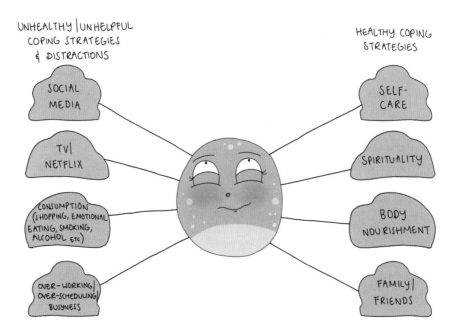

UNHEALTHY |UNHELPFUL COPING STRATEGIES & DISTRACTIONS

HEALTHY COPING STRATEGIES

SOCIAL MEDIA

TV| NETFLIX

CONSUMPTION (SHOPPING, EMOTIONAL EATING, SMOKING, ALCOHOL ETC)

OVER-WORKING| OVER-SCHEDULING| BUSYNESS

SELF-CARE

SPIRITUALITY

BODY NOURISHMENT

FAMILY| FRIENDS

Down the left side, you'll see a list of unhealthy coping strategies/ distractions for you to write in the rocks. If any of these unhelpful coping strategies don't apply to you, feel free to sub them out for something else or add your own unhelpful go-to strategies as additional rocks. Many clients sub in things like 'going into an unhelpful thinking spiral', for example. Down the right side, you'll see a list of healthy coping strategies inside rocks. If any of these don't apply to you or you have any others that are particularly meaningful, please feel free to sub out or add in.

Here are the instructions for this exercise. First, go around each coping strategy and mark a dash along the guideline that represents how much you value this coping strategy or how important it is to you. For example, if the coping strategy is highly important, you would mark a dash right next to the rock. If the coping strategy isn't important to you/you don't value it at all, your dash would be close to the octopus body.

Next, go around and draw a tentacle that represents how much time you spend on that coping strategy. For example, if you spend a lot of time on social media you would draw a tentacle that reached right up to the rock. If you don't spend very much time on self-care, that tentacle is going to look rather unfortunate and stubby!

Now that you have filled in your dashes and tentacles, you can reflect on these points:

- How much disparity is there between how much you value a coping strategy versus how much time you actually spend on that coping strategy?

- How do you feel about where you are spending your most time?

- If you were to live in alignment with your values/spend time on the things you value the most, which coping strategies would you need to put more effort into?

Here is an example of a filled-in octopus:

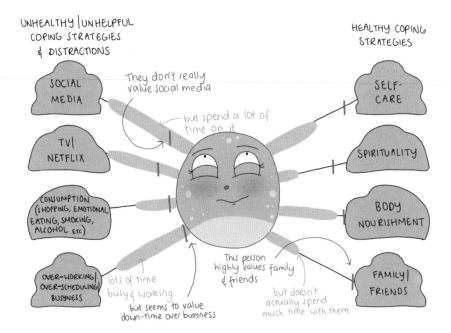

UNHEALTHY |UNHELPFUL COPING STRATEGIES & DISTRACTIONS

HEALTHY COPING STRATEGIES

SOCIAL MEDIA

TV| NETFLIX

CONSUMPTION (SHOPPING, EMOTIONAL EATING, SMOKING, ALCOHOL ETC)

OVER-WORKING/ OVER-SCHEDULING/ BUSYNESS

SELF-CARE

SPIRITUALITY

BODY NOURISHMENT

FAMILY| FRIENDS

They don't really value social media

but spend a lot of time on it

This person highly values family & friends

lots of time busy & working

but seems to value down-time over busyness

but doesn't actually spend much time with them

Reflections:

- Realises they need to invest more time into family and friends in particular

- Would cling to social media, TV, work and body nourishment in tough times

- Reflects on shifting priorities to spend less time working and scrolling and more time on self-care

It isn't enough just to value things that are good for us.

The moral of the story is that when the sea gets rough and choppy and life gets hard for the octopus, he will cling on to the things that he has the strongest connection with at the time. In other words, if his tentacles are wrapped around the rocks that represent unhealthy coping strategies and distractions, because that is what he spends the most time doing, then when times get tough that is what he will rely on to get through.

It isn't enough just to value things that are good for us. We have to put the time and effort into the coping strategies that are important and the things that we know will nourish us, even when times are good. This way we have a solid connection so that when times get rough and life is difficult, we will lean on things that serve and support our wellbeing.

If right now you spend a lot of time working, scrolling social media or ruminating on negative thoughts, then when times get tough those are the exact things that you will revert to in order to get through. It won't be self-care or your family that you turn to, because your connection isn't strong and you haven't practised those things.

So, ask yourself: when the sea gets rough in your life, and times get tough, what is it that you will be clinging to?

Perfectionism

If you identify as a perfectionist, you are not alone. You might have realised that this tendency of yours has become rather limiting; something that might be sabotaging your efforts to be your best self. In this section we're going to look at the three types of perfectionist, some of the things that might be behind your perfectionist traits, and some of the paths out of perfectionism.

First, let me say that there may not be any problem with being a bit of a perfectionist! And if you find that it doesn't get in your way or feed into struggles with your sense of self-worth, then all power to you! You probably don't feel like you need to change or work on this. Take my husband, for example: a total perfectionist in his work — but not to his detriment. It serves him well, and work ethic matters to him. His perfectionism also applies to him thinking my way of doing the dishes is incorrect . . . but thankfully he doesn't nag me about this. Our marriage survives my less-than-perfect housekeeping skills and he hasn't developed a nervous eye twitch (yet). So we can let his perfectionism slide!

BUT so many of the people I work with describe to me how debilitating their perfectionist traits are. They find that it feeds into their sense of worth as a person, and they struggle with control and being incredibly hard on themselves or others in their lives.

I do not need to make sure everything is perfect in order to be loved, accepted or to have control.

Which type of perfectionist are you?

What are the three types of perfectionist?

1. **The people-pleaser**
   - Feels immense pressure to 'live up to' the expectations of others.
   - Often seeks approval.
   - Believes they need to be perfect to be worthy or accepted by others.
   - Worries about others rejecting or disapproving of them.
   - May feel rejected if criticised.
   - Gets caught up in 'mind reading' thinking styles.
   - Believes others hold high expectations of them.
   - Puts the needs and happiness of others above their own.

2. **The high-standards holder**
   - Expects perfection from others.
   - Extremely high standards for those around them.
   - Critical and judgemental of others.
   - May experience relationship problems.
   - Has been called 'picky' or 'impossible to please'.
   - Finds it hard to delegate tasks because 'no one else can do it right'.

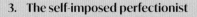

3. The self-imposed perfectionist

- Sets themselves unrealistically difficult goals.
- Puts immense pressure on themselves.
- Extremely high standards of self.
- Sees failure as losing.
- Own sense of esteem and worth tied up in achievement.

- Very hard on self.
- Gets caught up in black-and-white thinking and catastrophising.
- Prone to burnout and stress.
- Prone to procrastination.
- Thinks nothing they do is good enough.

* Many people find they are some combination of the three styles, while likely being dominant in an area. You can go through the three types of perfectionist and highlight any of the traits you notice in yourself.

What causes perfectionism?

Many perfectionists have a limiting core belief that unless something is perfect, they themselves are not acceptable or worthy as a person. Others believe that when things aren't perfect they have lost control, and cannot cope with the discomfort that this brings. So how does one come to be a perfectionist? What causes these traits? Let's explore some of the possibilities. Do you resonate with any of these?

- You grew up with parents who were overly critical, abusive or shamed you for your mistakes or performance. If your achievement was anything less than perfect, this was pointed out to you. It felt like you could never do anything right and nothing you did was up to their demands and standards.

- Growing up you needed to be the 'perfect' child. You had to be the 'easy one'. Maybe this was because:

- Your parents only paid you attention if you acted this way.

- Your parents were harsh or abusive, and you needed to be perfect and easy in order to be safe.

- You had a sibling who was 'difficult' for some reason and you felt you had to make things easy on your parents; they just didn't have the time or energy for you to be anything other than perfect.

- You find that your own self-worth is tied up in achievement. For you, the most important things are academic success, how much money you earn, your job title, your relationship status and so on — if you don't have these accolades, you feel like you are failing and are somehow 'less than' others.

> Many perfectionists have a limiting core belief that unless something is perfect, they themselves are not acceptable or worthy as a person.

- You are afraid. Perfectionism is often driven by fear. You think, consciously or otherwise, that you can avoid judgement, pain, shame, blame, rejection, failure and vulnerability if you are perfect. Some part of you feels you just can't cope with the discomfort that comes with these things.

- Doing things perfectly temporarily provides a sense of comfort and relieves anxiety. It feels like you have control and you are provided with short-term relief and soothing. The key words here being 'short-term'.

- You have unrealistic standards. Either you expect far more of yourself than you would of others in your life, or you expect far too much of others; there needs to be room for humanness and mistakes. This might develop from experiencing failures or being let down in the past.

- Growing up, you were overly praised for your achievements and 'success' was a marker of your worth. When you excelled, won an award or nailed a test, you were drowned in praise. When you weren't winning, there may not have been much attention or recognition at all. You learnt that you needed to be perfect to be worthy of connection and to be seen.

- You're trying to feel in control. You're a person who likes to have all your ducks in a row. This may come from experiencing a trauma. Or from having no control during a difficult time in your life; after this, the pendulum swung in the opposite direction, and now things feel threatening or unsafe for you if they aren't perfect and predictable.

- You find yourself in spirals of unhelpful thinking styles, like mind reading, catastrophising and black-and-white thinking. These biased thinking styles can lend themselves to perfectionist behaviours.

- You believe you aren't good enough, or that things aren't worth doing if they aren't perfect.

How do you overcome perfectionism?

Here's a hint about the challenges and tools to come: they all involve getting used to the discomfort of not doing things perfectly (stay with me!). First let's look at the individual goals for the three types of perfectionist and then explore some general tools.

The goal of the people-pleaser

You need to remember that your worth is not determined by what other people think of you (especially when you're only guessing what they think — remember that mind-reading thinking style?!). Your goal is to shift your self-evaluation to be internal. This means that you are the one whose opinion matters the most. You are innately worthy and this worth does not diminish or ebb and flow based on your achievements or ability to be perfect. Set yourself some clear boundaries and prioritise your own needs and values.

The goal of the high-standards holder

It's time to get realistic about your expectations of others. Evaluate how your high expectations are affecting those around you and the relationships in your life. Your goal is to learn to sit with the discomfort of allowing others to make mistakes and be imperfect. Focus only on things that are within your control — you cannot control others. And yes, this means letting your partner stack the dishwasher 'wrong'!

The goal of the self-imposed perfectionist

You need to remember your worth is NOT determined by achievement. You are an innately worthy and valuable human, exactly as you are. Adopt the mantra 'practice makes progress' and let go of unrealistic self-imposed expectations. Don't expect more of yourself than you do of others. Practise tasks you can't do perfectly and sit in the discomfort that brings.

One way of getting comfortable with the discomfort of lowering your standards and moving away from perfectionist traits is to get used to not doing everything perfectly. Remember that the relief you feel when things are 'perfect' is temporary. That means this vulnerable and uncomfortable feeling is going to come right back around again. You'll never be free of it, as there is always another task or thing that 'needs to be perfect'. The freedom comes from letting go, cutting yourself some slack, making mistakes . . . and leaving things a mess sometimes!

You can do this by practising exposure techniques. This means you expose yourself to tasks that you do imperfectly on purpose. Here are some ideas of things you could do imperfectly on purpose:

Get up in the morning and don't make the bed.

Leave the dishes on the bench until the morning.

Send an email without proofreading it.

Bake a cake without the recipe.

Go to a dance class if you can't dance.

Finger-paint or, better yet, do it with your elbows — that'll be a right mess!

The idea here is to do any task that you usually do perfectly, and do it imperfectly. Or to try a brand-new task just for fun; not for the perfect outcome. Stop when it isn't 100 per cent right and sit with the discomfort that brings.

The goal here is not in the outcome. It's in the process. It's allowing things just to be and allowing yourself to feel a little bit of that discomfort you've been trying to avoid. You're doing it right if you are feeling uncomfortable!

Case study

Casey was one of my group-coaching clients. During a session I asked, 'Does anyone here identify as having perfectionist traits that get in the way?' The hands of most of the group sprung up into the view of the many little screens on Zoom, Casey's most furiously. We began to discuss perfectionism and how it might occur. Casey nodded along, suddenly making the connection that she had been through a difficult and traumatic time a few years back and ever since then she'd struggled to let go of control; everything had to be 'perfect', everything had to be in its place. This was fuelled by the belief that if she didn't have full control, then she would lose control completely, and this would be unbearable. She was ready to let go of this — the need for perfection had taken over somewhat, and was causing a great deal of anxiety. It also meant that she often procrastinated starting projects, or didn't even start at all, for fear it wouldn't go perfectly (for more on procrastination, see pages 102–113).

We went through the list from above with ideas of things to do imperfectly. Casey — along with several others — was cringing at the thought of trying them out. We set the 'homework' that they would try to do some of the things from the list or try out some ideas of their own.

The next week, the group met again via Zoom and I asked how they had got on. One of our members had created some bespoke pottery (imperfectly wonky). Another an abstract art piece. One had let her son cook dinner (usually she couldn't stand the mess and the dinner not being the way she would do it, but she rejoiced that she survived the meal without food poisoning!) Casey shared her success; she had left the house one day without straightening the pillows on the couch (she revealed that she felt her house should look 'open-home ready' at all times), and she had left some dishes out one night.

So what did Casey learn from this? 'I didn't die!' she laughed. Casey (along with the others) had discovered that nothing bad happened as a result of letting go a little. And that she could cope with the feeling of not being perfect, too. While these may seem like small or simple steps, they are the 'perfect' way to start the exposure practice and to begin getting comfortable with being imperfectly human.

I am safe, accepted & valuable in my imperfection

Here are some reflection questions for you to further unpack perfectionism:

- 'Where might my perfectionist traits have come from?' (Think about your upbringing; events in your childhood, parental expectations and so on.)
- 'Who is my perfectionism serving?'
- 'Who is affected by my perfectionism and how?'
- 'What do I think will happen if things don't go perfectly/I am not perfect?'
- 'What do I stand to gain from letting go of perfectionism?'

Now, go forth . . . be messy. Be human. Experiment. Lean into discomfort and trust that your fabulously imperfect self is more than enough.

Procrastination

Can you relate to this? You have a huge project due. You sit down at your computer to begin, coffee at your side, focused, relaxation music on, door shut, ready to go. Forty-five minutes later you 'come to' from your daze and realise you have been on Pinterest virtually redesigning your living room decor for nearly an hour, while your work project sat unattended. You shake your head and click open a Word document, ready to get started now. But . . . you're a little hungry . . . you think, 'I should probably grab a quick bite to eat so I'm not unfocused; this project is important!' After you eat, you begin cleaning up the kitchen. You realise what a mess the pantry is and decide to clear out a few half-empty jars and wipe down the shelves. An hour later, you find yourself on the floor in the garage going through old photos from 1992 wondering how on earth you got there and feeling even more overwhelmed by your project that is still waiting for you to start.

> Procrastination can be a major
> way we self-sabotage.

Procrastination can be a major way we self-sabotage. In a recent poll on Instagram, I asked my audience, 'Do you procrastinate?' A whopping 92 per cent of respondents said yes. So, if you are a master procrastinator, join the crew! You are NOT alone. I then asked, 'If you said yes, what do you put that down to?' Here is what the pollers said.

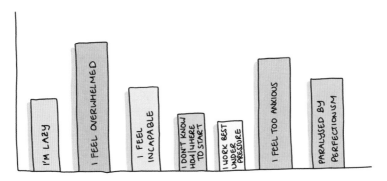

Why do you procrastinate?

Let's break down these reasons for procrastination and look at some tools that could help.

Being lazy

I am going to stop you right there. Interestingly, in my Instagram poll 30 per cent of you said you procrastinate because you are lazy. The chances are, this just isn't true. And if you have said this, you may well have just uncovered a limiting core belief. Being lazy might be your excuse, or the tip of the iceberg. What lies underneath this is usually a lack of belief in self, or a lack of resources. Even if you simply hold the unhelpful belief 'I am lazy', you are going to hinder your own progress and get in your own way.

Overwhelm/lacking motivation/don't know where to start

'I just don't know where to start!' or, 'I just don't have any motivation to do it.' I hear this from clients often — actually, I hear this from my own brain often, too! Motivation, or lack thereof, and overwhelm are major stumbling blocks when it comes to getting your A into G (ass into gear).

Here's the deal: action comes before motivation. Not the other way around. If we sit and wait for motivation to show up so that we can get started on a task, it probably won't come. What can really help with this sounds simple: just start. I know, I know . . . ! If only it were that easy. But it's actually a wonderful tool to get the ball rolling. If you can just start the thing you are putting off — take one small step, and continue putting one foot in front of the other — this action will actually build into more action and eventually snowball into some form of motivation.

Now, if motivation is at an all-time low, you may be able to trick your mind by getting started on something else first and segueing over to the task you are putting off. If you can just get that action piece going on something small and easy, this may be enough to put an end to you feeling paralysed. For example, have to pack up your whole house to move but you're stuck on the couch in your pyjamas staring at a wall? Jump up, get changed and do your hair. That small achievement may kick-start your flow.

Here's another great trick: the five-second rule. If you have a thought about doing something, act on that thought in some way within five seconds. You see, when you don't take action quickly you tend to talk yourself out of it. Here's an example of what happens without action — a super-common one for me!

> *I'm mucking around home and I have the thought 'I should really get outside, and take my daughter and the dog for a walk.' I pause for a second. I look around the lounge. Then I think, 'I can't really be bothered right now, though.' Then I think, 'No, come on, we need to get out.' I'm still sitting on the couch at this point. Now I'm thinking, 'Hmm, it's kind of windy. That's not nice. Maybe we'll just stay home until later.' Later comes, and I do not walk. And then I feel guilty. (Hello, inner critic!)*

We have to break down tasks that seem overwhelming or unachievable into small and manageable chunks.

Here is the same scenario using the five-second rule.

I'm mucking around home and I have the thought, 'I should really get outside, and take my daughter and the dog for a walk.' I instantly stand up, stride over to the door and begin putting on my sneakers. I call out to my daughter and dog, 'Let's go for a walk, team!' Then I think, 'Oh man, I can't be bothered!' But it's too late — the shoes are on and the kids (one human, one fur) are pumped to get outside. I feel I have no choice but to follow through now, so we get out and we walk. Afterwards I feel pleased with myself for getting off my butt and doing it. This then goes against any beliefs I might have about being lazy or not following through on things; now I am building evidence for a new core belief. Win!

One last thing to consider if overwhelm is the biggest part of your procrastination: if you were a person who had never run before, you wouldn't suddenly go and partake in a marathon, would you? No. You might begin by running five minutes a day, slowly and steadily building your way up. We have to break down tasks that seem overwhelming or unachievable into small and manageable chunks. For example, if you are moving house, the thought of packing everything up feels enormous. So you break it down like this: Pack whole house > Pack kitchen > Pack pot drawer/pack cutlery/pack pantry, and so on. Once you have your larger task broken down into smaller chunks, you can then schedule in those chunks, creating and carving out time in your diary to tackle them one by one.

You can also set yourself time-trials or time-limits. For instance, 'I will spend exactly 30 minutes packing right now', or 'I have 30 minutes to get all the cutlery, pots and glasses packed. One, two, three . . . GO!' If even 30 minutes feels like too much for the level of overwhelm you are experiencing, you can set a timer for just five minutes, starting small and manageable and checking in with yourself after five minutes to see if some motivation has been sparked. Even if it hasn't, you've still achieved five minutes! Still overwhelmed? The tool in this next section is for you.

Feeling incapable

When it comes to procrastination, there are often limiting core beliefs that get in the way and act as a handbrake to us getting started on tasks. Feeling incapable or not good enough are examples of a limiting core belief getting in the way. You can imagine how a belief like 'I am a failure', 'I never stick to things' or 'I can't do hard things' might hold you back and feed in to procrastination behaviour, creating a self-fulfilling prophecy.

If you are procrastinating for these reasons, head to pages 145-149 and begin the work of unpacking and re-writing some of these beliefs. And remember: not all thoughts and beliefs are true! If you want to re-write these, you have got to do the work in building up examples for yourself of you sticking to things, getting things done and having some success. This doesn't have to go smoothly and look perfect at the end. It just has to be you showing up for yourself and getting stuck in.

If you're feeling incapable because the task itself just feels too hard, then break it down into small, manageable and achievable chunks and recruit support and help — you don't have to do hard things alone.

Best under pressure

If you are someone who procrastinates and procrastinates then eventually pulls the whole thing together at the very last minute, and if that works for you, then all power to you! Carry on! Some people just work best like this.

If this strategy does work for you but you are also beating yourself up, drop the guilt and expectations and just go with it. BUT if you are doing this and it doesn't work for you, causing you anxiety, stress and overwhelm, here is another tool you can try out. This gives you that 'time-trial' style of pressure that you're used to, without the angst. I call it the 'Get Sh*t Done Tool' — catchy, right? Here's how it works.

Step 1: Draw yourself a time grid with six boxes, like this:

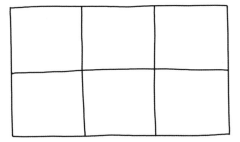

Step 2: Decide how much time each box represents. I usually do ten minutes, so that the whole grid represents an hour. But

if you need to put your head down and focus for longer, you could make each box fifteen or twenty minutes (making the whole grid one-and-a-half to two hours).

Step 3: Write out what you need to get done (your to-do list), and then prioritise the tasks. If there are big tasks, break them down into manageable chunks.

Step 4: Plot your to-do items into the grid. It's up to you how long you give to each task, and you can schedule the same task across multiple boxes. You can stay focused on one thing or, if you know the task is boring and hard to focus on, you can break it up with other items on your to-do list.

Step 5: Make sure you also use blocks in your grid as 'free time', so it feels like you are being rewarded along the way — and so you have something to look forward to and work towards.

Step 6: When you are ready to start block one, set a timer on your phone for the block length (e.g. ten minutes) and then GO!

Step 7: Work as efficiently as you possibly can, staying laser-focused for that ten-minute block. When the timer goes off, reset it for the next block and get cracking on the tasks in that one.

At the end, you will have efficiently and effectively worked through a full grid of tasks.

This tool truly helps me stay extremely focused. I use it often when I have a bunch of 'home admin' to get done but I am procrastinating because I just can't be bothered. Here is how my last grid of home admin looked.

I broke the emails up into separate time chunks, because I knew I was in no mood for them that day. Knowing I only had ten minutes meant I was more likely to stay focused. I gave myself a break for a cup of tea near the end. I worked at lightning speed and it felt like I was in some kind of exciting race, a kind of 'Hunger Games for housewives' mission, even though I was really just scrubbing the loo!

A little hint: when you are using the Get Sh*t Done Tool with work that requires a lot of concentration and mental energy, be mindful not to switch between tasks too often — as you switch, you lose a little of your focus and efficiency each time.

Anxiety/fear

Sometimes you procrastinate because you feel anxious or fearful of starting. Maybe you are putting off a big decision, a major lifestyle change, going to therapy . . . There are so many things that seem scary and send you into an anxious tailspin.

Remember that ancient caveman brain of yours? It's trying to protect you — something new or unfamiliar or overwhelming can trigger your threat response. Even though you are technically safe, your brain might not think so. It will naturally make you think of all the possible worst-case scenarios and activate a whole range of uncomfortable (but normal) symptoms in your body.

Remember pages 76–83, where we talked about avoidance? Well, this applies here, too — you are avoiding something when you procrastinate. Only this type of avoidance might not offer a feeling of relief. You might feel overwhelming worry and anxiety that only increases the longer you postpone the inevitable. You will need to lean into the discomfort and the anxiety. Putting off starting will only cement and extend your anxiety in the long run.

Perfectionism

If you have the belief that everything needs to be perfect, it will feel totally overwhelming to begin a task. You might put it off — or decide not to do it at all! If this is the case for you, you'll definitely want to head back to pages 92–101 and get cracking on that perfectionist side of yours. For you perfectionists out there, remember this:

- Things do NOT have to be perfect.

- Imperfect and finished is better than not done at all (there is a high chance the perfectionist in you is rolling their eyes or screaming 'NO IT ISN'T!' at this one . . . if so, do some of that deep unpacking work around where this belief might come from and how well it is serving you).

- Adopt the mantra 'practice makes progress', not 'practice makes perfect'.

- Tell yourself, 'This is an old and unhelpful belief that I can let go of. I can choose to act in a different way.'

- Exposure to imperfection is a part of the work. Do it imperfectly on purpose.

Before we sign off on our procrastination chapter, I have three more points to make.

1. Remember your inner critic! Remember how it has the knack of being sickly sweet and manipulating you into doing things that are against your best interests. Your inner critic works in the same way when it baits you into procrastination. It will tell you all kinds of things you could be doing instead of the one thing that you 'should' be doing. Your inner critic thinks it is a GREAT idea to start a new Netflix series instead of completing that project; it loves the idea of painting your nails instead of having that hard conversation with your partner; oh, and what a fabulous plan to clean out all the things in your attic space right now instead of doing your end-of-year taxes! Of course, right after this stuff, when it's now too late in the day to do what you're meant to be doing, it will turn around and berate you for being lazy and useless and never sticking to tasks.

2. Be mindful of 'busy-work' that doesn't align with your values, and distracts from your goals or what you 'should' be doing. Busy-work can include cleaning, emails, work admin, errands . . . pretty much anything that might actually need to be done — but doesn't need to be done instead of the thing that is the main priority. Busy-work makes you feel like you can't possibly be procrastinating because you are doing work, right? But this is actually just a smokescreen — your way of getting out of doing what really matters. Maybe because you're overwhelmed, or maybe because your limiting beliefs have reared their ugly heads. Notice when you are doing this, and delegate this work to others where you can. Work first on your urgent and important task, then on the important but not urgent ones.

3. Keep in mind that your brain loves to revert to autopilot. It will always want to choose the thing that feels the most comfortable and familiar rather than something that feels new, threatening or difficult. This means that your brain will choose your comfort zone over whatever it is that you are procrastinating about — Netflix over going out to a social event, cleaning the kitchen over that big project that's due for work, and so on. Your brain may even choose things that are unhealthy or painful to you, if they are familiar. To your brain, this 'known pain' is still more comfortable than the discomfort of the unknown.

Summary

- Your brain loves familiarity, taking the easiest path and instant gratification.

- Many of the unhealthy coping strategies or distractions we engage in just feel easier for our brains.

- We have to put intentional time in to building healthy habits that we value.

- Perfectionism can often develop from childhood, trauma, or needing control or fear.

- In order to break free from perfectionism, remember to check your standards and do things imperfectly on purpose.

- Procrastination isn't usually about laziness. Work on the real cause of your procrastination.

- Remember that motivation doesn't come first. Break things down into small, time-measured and manageable steps and take action first to build momentum and motivation.

TAME YOUR THOUGHTS

The way you think has an influence over how you feel and behave — this is especially true and unhelpful when you buy into every unkind thought you have. It's time to tame your thoughts — let's discover how to spot those sticky thinking styles that trip you up and learn how to sort fact from fiction.

The Thinking–Doing–Feeling Connection

Let's take a look at how Cognitive Behavioural Therapy (CBT) explains emotions, behaviour, thinking and change. You see, your feelings, your behaviour/actions and your thoughts are all interconnected, each one affecting the others and going around and around in a cycle. I'm sure most of us have wished at some point or another that there was a switch we could flick or a pill we could take to just stop feeling an uncomfortable emotion. Why can't we just turn off insecurity?! Surely there's some kind of cheat-code in a manual on 'How to Human' that we don't know about?!

The fact remains that you cannot switch your emotions on and off. What you can do, however, is make changes in one of the other areas of this triangle. You can change the way you think — or rather, the way you respond to your thoughts — and you can change the way you behave. In doing so, there is a natural flow-on effect, shifting the way you feel via these two other avenues.

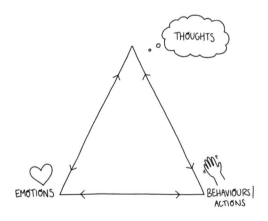

Let's look at an example of this interconnection at play when it comes to experiencing insecurity and low mood.

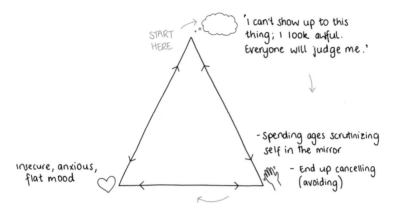

'I can't show up to this thing; I look awful. Everyone will judge me.'

START HERE

- Spending ages scrutinizing self in the mirror
- End up cancelling (avoiding)

Insecure, anxious, flat mood

You can see how this cycle would perpetuate and repeat itself. The more you avoid those social situations, the more your confidence in yourself drops. The lower your confidence gets, the more you think to yourself 'I can't cope', 'I can't do this' and so on. This is a common spiral that we find ourselves in as humans. We take our emotions to be facts, confusing them as some kind of proof that the negative thoughts we are experiencing are true.

So, what would happen if we made some subtle changes to our thinking and/or behaviours in this situation?

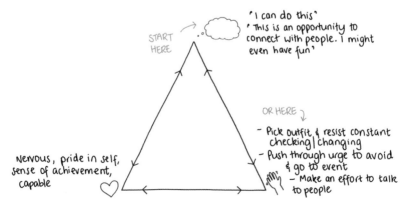

'I can do this'
'This is an opportunity to connect with people. I might even have fun'

START HERE

OR HERE

- Pick outfit & resist constant checking | changing
- Push through urge to avoid & go to event
- Make an effort to talk to people

Nervous, pride in self, sense of achievement, capable

Using this approach, you can unpack some of the tricky moments and emotions you are feeling to get a feel for how your thoughts and actions might be contributing to them. One way of doing this is to keep a log in response to moments of anxiety, insecurity or low mood. This helps you take a step back to hopefully objectively view a situation, uncover patterns and create some change.

Let's look at one example of how to keep a log. After pages 126–143 about challenging unhelpful thoughts, we will go one step further with this log: challenging and re-writing our thoughts and re-evaluating our actions and emotions. But first, meet Jane.

Case study

Jane was in her early thirties and had been in several 'rocky' relationships prior to meeting her current partner of two years, Naomi. Naomi was committed and supportive, but Jane was struggling with her inner critic and insecurities. She often felt low in the order of priorities for Naomi (a hang-up from previous relationships). Naomi had a high-stress job and wasn't available to answer calls during work days. Jane would find herself in the same arguments with Naomi, time and time again. Jane and I met in my counselling room on a rainy afternoon and she described their most recent blow-up. Jane had finished work and checked her phone. Seeing her notifications were empty, she began her drive home. Along the way, a spiral of thoughts began. She felt increasingly hurt and angry as she ruminated, chewing over thoughts like 'She never contacts me first' and 'I've obviously done something wrong'. Anticipating a frosty reception when Naomi got home, Jane fired off a sarcastic, passive-aggressive text: 'My day was fine, thanks for asking. So nice to hear from you today.' Still no reply.

By the time Naomi got home, Jane was angry and anxious. She opted for the silent treatment, leaving the room as a confused Naomi put down her bag, took her phone from a pocket and put it on charge; it had died earlier in the day. Naomi was bewildered and Jane felt terrible.

I've popped Jane's example into the thought log on the following page. I encourage you to draw up your own thought log in a journal and take the next couple of days to notice times that you feel a tricky emotion and log this down (in the emotion column), then ask yourself:

☆ ☆ ☆ ☆ ☆

- 'What was happening right before I noticed this feeling? What triggered this?' (Put this information in the trigger column.)

- 'What was I thinking at that moment? Which thoughts or images were in my mind?' (Put this information in the thoughts/beliefs column.)

- 'What did I do as a result? What was my response? How did I act?' (Put this information in the behaviours column.)

Trigger	*Didn't hear from partner today*
Emotion	*Hurt, insecure, anxious, mad*
Thought/belief	*'What have I done to annoy her?!'*
	'How dare she ignore me? That is so rude.'
	'She should be contacting me.'
	'I should just end the relationship. Nothing ever works for me, anyway.'
Behaviour	*Sent partner a passive-aggressive text*
	Ignored partner when she got home

There is a fifth column we can add here: consequences. What happened as a result of our unhelpful thinking styles and behaviours? Here's Jane's example. Add this column to your own log when you're ready to begin reflecting.

Trigger	*Didn't hear from partner today*
Emotion	*Hurt, insecure, anxious, mad*
Thought/ belief	*'What have I done to annoy her?!'* *'How dare she ignore me? That is so rude.'* *'She should be contacting me.'* *'I should just end the relationship. Nothing ever works for me, anyway.'*
Behaviour	*Sent partner a passive-aggressive text* *Ignored partner when she got home*
Consequence/ result	*Got in an argument with partner* *Felt guilty*

We are going to come back to Jane in the next two chapters as we unpack her thoughts and behaviours around this situation. Hopefully looking at these logs gives you a clear idea of how our emotions, thoughts and behaviours are all so heavily interconnected. So, how can we use this knowledge to our advantage to manage our emotions? Read on . . .

Unhelpful Thoughts

There are certain thinking styles that we all fall into now and again, resulting in us feeling worse than we 'need to'. The way we think and the way we think about our emotions plays a huge part in how we feel. While all of us experience these unhelpful thinking styles, we do so to varying degrees. It's normal to notice thoughts that fit into these unhelpful-thinking-style categories in your day. Sometimes they are insignificant and don't have much impact, other times we might experience them often, or get stuck and fixated on these ways of thinking — this becomes habitual and, of course, leads us down the track of feeling anxious, insecure or depressed.

What are the unhelpful thinking styles?

First, let's take a look at some of the most common unhelpful thinking styles we all experience from time to time (see opposite).

Right, now back to the thoughts in Jane's example on page 120. Let's look at these again:

- 'What have I done to annoy her?!'

- 'How dare she ignore me? That is so rude.'

- 'She should be contacting me.'

- 'I should just end the relationship. Nothing ever works for me, anyway.'

Which thinking styles do you see here?

- **'What have I done to annoy her?!'** There are two thinking styles at work here: mind reading and jumping to conclusions. Jane

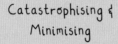

Unhelpful Thinking Styles

Catastrophising & Minimising

Blowing things out of proportion OR shrinking something to make it seem less important than it is

Jumping to Conclusions

Imagining you know what other people are thinking OR predicting what is going to happen. Lots of 'what ifs'

Emotional Reasoning

Assuming that because you feel a certain way, that whatever you are thinking must be true

Filtering

Only paying attention to certain types of evidence or focusing on the 'bad' over the good

'Should-ing'

Being critical, harsh & demanding of yourself. Saying 'I should' or 'I shouldn't' & feeling guilty or like a failure, OR 'shoulds' on others leading to frustration & resentment

Personalisation

Blaming yourself or taking responsibility for something that wasn't entirely your fault OR blaming other people for things you need to take ownership for

All or Nothing Thinking

Black & white thinking. When you view things in extremes; right or wrong, good or bad

Labelling

Assigning labels to yourself or others, often in the form of harsh & judgemental language or name-calling is assuming that Naomi is angry at her, but she doesn't know this for a fact. She is also assuming that she must have done something in order to warrant this perceived 'silent treatment' from Naomi.

- **'How dare she ignore me? That is so rude.'** Mind reading again here, Jane! And personalising, too — Naomi not texting her wasn't about Jane at all.

- **'She should be contacting me.'** Shoulding. When we use the word 'should' on ourselves or others, we are placing a level of expectation on something that often results in a sense of disappointment, shame or resentment. Here, Jane is 'shoulding on' Naomi; placing an expectation on Naomi's behaviour. This is based on what Jane thinks, but was never communicated as a need to Naomi. Naomi is in the dark on this unmet need of Jane's, and so is set up for failure.

- **'I should just end the relationship. Nothing ever works for me, anyway.'** Here Jane is catastrophising and stuck in black-and-white thinking. The situation and response have been blown out of proportion. The use of words like 'always', 'ever' or 'never' are a giveaway that all-or-nothing or black-and-white thinking is at play. Is it really true that nothing ever works out? And does she really need to consider leaving over this, or is she making a mountain out of a molehill? (And probably racing for an exit strategy to cope with all the icky anxiety and past-relationship memories.)

When you begin to observe your thinking, the chances are you'll be surprised by how often you notice unhelpful thinking styles at work.

It's so important to do this with compassion. Notice, acknowledge, but don't judge yourself harshly for having these thoughts. Remember, we all do. It's really normal. Shining a light on them can be daunting, but it can also be liberating. Yes, it might take some work to get out of the habit of these ways of thinking but, if you ask me, it's worth the effort!

The next column we will add to our thought log is identifying the thinking style.

Trigger	Didn't hear from partner today
Emotion	Hurt, insecure, anxious, mad
Thought/belief	'What have I done to annoy her?!' 'How dare she ignore me? That is so rude.' 'She should be contacting me.' 'I should just end the relationship. Nothing ever works for me, anyway.'
Thinking style	Future-predicting Mind reading and personalisation Shoulding Catastrophising and black-and-white thinking
Behaviour	Sent her a passive-aggressive text Ignored her when she got home

If you would like to continue unpacking your own thoughts, take the next few days to add this extra step in the log: identifying the unhelpful thinking style. When you've done that, meet me below to learn how to challenge those unhelpful thoughts.

P.S. I know you're totally going to just keep reading without pausing to do your log . . . I know it because that's what I do, too! It's okay, I get it. But I do encourage you at some point to give this thought-logging a go to see if it helps you with some lightbulb moments. We often think we can just do this stuff in our minds, but something profound happens when we put pen to paper.

How can you challenge unhelpful thoughts?

I tend to approach unhelpful thoughts in one of two ways: challenging and re-writing them, or using a mindful acceptance approach. We'll explore both of these avenues in this section. Let's start with the former — challenging and re-writing.

You've got to remember this: just because you have a thought does not make it true. Your thoughts are not facts.

Some of your thoughts are conscious; you have them on purpose. Some of them seem to come out of nowhere or happen very automatically, as though your mind is on autopilot and you have no say in what comes up. These thoughts can often be the unhelpful ones, the inner critic ones, even the intrusive ones. With the exception of your intrusive thoughts (which are junk thoughts that don't deserve the airtime or our buy-in), one way of responding to unhelpful thoughts that pop up is to challenge the little pests. You don't have to just helplessly believe them. You are the author of your own story; it's time to get out your pencil and make some revisions!

> You are the author of your own story; it's time to get out your pencil and make some revisions!

To challenge your thoughts, you can ask yourself questions and use the answers to help you re-write the thought into something new. You challenge unhelpful thinking styles in the same way you challenge your inner critic, so head back to the first chapter to review this.

Remember, there are key conditions of your new, re-written thought. It needs to be:

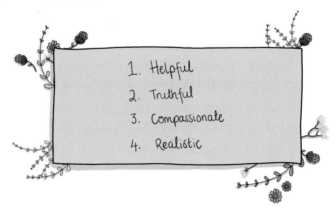

1. Helpful
2. Truthful
3. Compassionate
4. Realistic

Here is a list of questions you can use to challenge your unhelpful thoughts:

Challenge Your Unhelpful Thoughts

Am I confusing this thought with a fact?

Am I over-generalising?

Am I taking something too personally or taking responsibility for something I don't need to?

Am I filtering out the positive and focusing on the negative?

Am I assuming that my view of things is the only one possible?

Is this a double standard? Would I say this to a friend?

Am I catastrophising?

Am I over-generalising?

Am I assuming I have no control of influence to change my situation?

Am I concentrating on my weak points and ignoring my strengths?

What is more helpful, compassionate or realistic thought?

Am I predicting the future or assuming I know what others are thinking?

Am I ruminating on how things 'should be' instead of accepting and dealing with reality?

When you have asked yourself the challenge questions, try re-writing your unhelpful thought. Remember: helpfulness, truth, compassion, realism. When we re-write a thought, the idea is to do it in real-time — before the old, unhelpful behaviour and responses to that thought and to our tricky emotions occurs. Catch yourself when you notice that surge of anxiety, anger or insecurity, and then consider the thoughts you are having. Ask yourself, 'What am I thinking in this moment?' And then challenge and re-write those thoughts. This is going to impact how you feel, and create some space and breathing room to change your response, too.

Let's add another column to our thought log for new thoughts, and remove the thinking style and old behaviour columns, replacing them with your new response/behaviour. We'll revisit Jane's example, re-writing her thoughts and seeing how this might impact her behaviour.

Trigger	*Didn't hear from partner today*
Emotion	*Hurt, insecure, anxious, mad*
Original thought/ belief	*'What have I done to annoy her?!'* *'How dare she ignore me? That is so rude.'* *'She should be contacting me.'* *'I should just end the relationship. Nothing ever works for me, anyway.'*

New thought	*'Chances are I haven't done anything to annoy her. I can check that out with her later if I need to.'*
	'I know Naomi has a demanding job. I will hear from her when she is free.'
	'I have communicated my needs for contact with Naomi, and we have compromised with the solution of spending 30 minutes of quality time together in the evenings after work.'
	'While past relationships may not have worked out, this is not then. I am here now and I am putting in the work for a healthy relationship.'
New behaviour	*Clearly communicate feelings with Naomi.*
	Compromise on contact during the day.
	Set aside quality time.
	Allow Naomi space in the day.
	Sit and do a breathing or mindfulness practice when old core belief is triggered.
	Write a list of all the things that remind me I am good enough.
	Journal on/fill in thought log when unhelpful thoughts arise.

Changing your response to your thoughts — and re-writing them when they are unhelpful and riddled with bias and unhelpful thinking styles — has a powerful flow-on effect, shifting the way you feel and releasing you from old patterns and behaviours that just aren't working for you.

This is just one of the two approaches to thoughts that we'll look at in this chapter. The other is a mindful acceptance approach. And yes, you can absolutely do both. Let's explore a mindful approach.

First off, so we're all on the same page, mindfulness is about becoming aware of your thoughts, emotions, physical sensations and overall experience, in the present moment, without judgement.

Creating this space between you and the thought helps disentangle you from the web of lies we are pulled into by our insecurities and anxieties. This approach works in the same way for your emotions, too: 'I am here to witness and observe my emotions.' You aren't trying to change thoughts, to push them away or judge them. Nor are you trying to fix or fight your emotions.

Imagine it like this: your thoughts (and emotions) are snowflakes, hundreds of them swirling around in a flurry. When you follow every thought, every feeling, believing and attaching to each one, you are effectively standing out in a snowstorm. It's hard to see clearly.

A mindful acceptance approach is this: you step inside, out of the snowstorm. You sit by the cosy fire and look out of the window at the snowflakes falling. It is still snowing — you cannot turn the snowstorm off (just like we cannot click our fingers to change our emotions and thoughts). But what you can do is step back to find some perspective and a little peace from the storm.

Using the 'and that's okay' tool from page 44 is a great way to try the mindful acceptance approach to your thoughts. When a thought pops up, simply notice it and add 'and that's okay' to the end of it.

You might also like to try adding this statement on to the beginning of your thoughts: 'I am noticing a thought about . . .', e.g. 'I am noticing a thought about not being good enough.' Or you can add 'and that is just a thought, not a fact' to the end, e.g. 'I never get anything done . . . and that is just a thought, not a fact.'

When you judge your thoughts, it's quite easy for them to begin to spiral. You've probably had that experience with self-doubt or anxiety before. The thought pops up, 'What if I can't do this?' Then, you think, 'Oh gosh, I might fail.' Then, 'That will be humiliating.' And then, 'I'm so useless — what is wrong with me?!' and so on.

A mindful acceptance approach simply acknowledges the thought at the top of the spiral and decides not to engage in a conversation with it. If the spiral continues anyway, we sit back and observe, not judging and not buying in. You might like to try this approach by doing the following.

- Imagine thoughts are leaves on a stem. They float into view, then float on by with the moving current.

- Imagine thoughts are raindrops on a window pane. They appear, and then slide away when they are ready.

- Imagine thoughts are clouds in the sky. They drift into sight and disappear again, into the horizon.

Try a mindful meditation by using one of the visualisations above and simply sitting, eyes closed and observing your thoughts as they come and go. Notice each one, watch it appear and then watch it disappear, replaced by another. Try not to wander off with them into a daydream, but if you do, know that it's normal and human and gently bring your focus back to the observation. You can use your breath as an 'anchor' to the present and to the meditation by noticing and observing it too, coming back to witness your inhale and exhale whenever your mind wanders.

Before we close this chapter, I wanted to address some common misconceptions about thoughts.

You think: *'I can control my thoughts.'*
Truth: *You can't! Thoughts randomly pop into our heads that are out of our control all the time. Much of what you think comes about unconsciously. You can certainly will some thoughts into your mind, but it's impossible to control all of your thoughts. Thinking that you can control them leads to frustration, self-judgement and discomfort.*

You think: *'My thoughts define my character.'*
Truth: *Your thoughts don't define you. Your chosen actions do. We have no control over random thoughts — only over what we do.*

You think: *'Because I have a thought (or an emotional reaction*

to one), it needs my attention. I need to examine and solve it.'
Truth: *Thoughts sometimes seem like they need our attention because of the emotional impact they have on us. The truth is that not all thoughts are worthy of attention. Not all thoughts are facts. Not all thoughts need to be followed or bought into. Just as the thought 'my eye twitched' doesn't require any extra attention from us, your inner critic or negative thoughts are the same. Some thoughts are just junk thoughts and they aren't worthy of arguing with, examining or even challenging at times, because doing so only fuels them.*

You think: *'My worries change probabilities in the real world.'*
Truth: *No matter how much you worry about something, it doesn't make it more or less likely to happen.*

You think: *'If my thought repeats, it must be significant.'*
Truth: *Nope! Thoughts tend to repeat if pushed away. Remember: what you resist persists (see page 41). A thought that keeps popping up doesn't indicate how important the thought is; it just indicates that it's stuck, and this might be because you are fighting it, trying too hard to reject it or fixating on it.*

You think: *'All my thoughts are true.'*
Truth: *Thoughts are not facts. Not everything you think is true or helpful — especially the unhelpful thinking styles and inner critic ones!*

What is sticky thinking?

It helped me immensely when I learnt that there are actually certain 'conditions' where our brain becomes more vulnerable to negative thinking. These are the times we are more likely to follow our inner critic down a rabbit hole, and get caught in a tug of war with our worry part or spiral into our insecurities. I call this 'sticky thinking': the times when your brain is more vulnerable to unhelpful thoughts. During these times, your thoughts are more likely to get stuck on repeat, and your threat response is more likely to be triggered.

So, under which conditions is your brain more prone to getting thoughts stuck?

- When you are hormonal (i.e. at certain times in your menstrual cycle, for those with ovaries).
- If you've had too much caffeine.
- If you are tired.
- When you have a hangover.
- If you are under a lot of stress.
- When you're experiencing anxiety or depression.
- Last thing at night when you're trying to sleep.
- First thing in the morning when you wake up.

All of these conditions make it more likely that a thought will get stuck and set off your alarm system.

Looking at the list above, can you identify times when you experience more unhelpful thoughts? If you can pinpoint a time when your brain is more sticky, you can set up measures to support yourself. For instance, if your inner critic gets loud close to the start of your cycle, you could increase your self-care in the week leading up to this — book in a massage, be mindful of how much work you take on, get intentional about down-time, go for gentle walks and pop Post-it notes around the house with some comforting affirmations. If your worries get stuck on repeat last thing in the evening, create a night-time routine: no screen time before bed, a relaxing hot shower with a couple of drops of essential oil on a cloth covering the drain, time to jot down some thoughts in a journal, a chamomile tea and a guided meditation while lying in bed. If you find yourself overly negative when you are tired, take active steps to work on your 'sleep hygiene' (healthy habits to support a good night's sleep), make time for self-care/down-time and get the rest you need.

At times when you feel flooded by unhelpful thoughts, ask yourself: 'Is my brain sticky right now? Am I tired? Stressed? Hormonal? Hungover? Is it first thing in the morning or last thing at night? Have I had too much coffee? Am I particularly anxious or down right now?' If you answer 'yes' to any of these questions, then you know that the things you are ruminating on in this moment are likely to be sticky thoughts that are not helpful to you. When you know this, you can take these thoughts with a grain of salt, increase your self-compassion, challenge the thoughts or mindfully observe them and allow them to pass by.

What are some fun ways to approach unhelpful thoughts?

These are some of my favourite ways to approach unhelpful thoughts. They require a lot less time and energy than challenging the thoughts (and who isn't all about efficiency?!) and they're a funky take on a mindful acceptance approach — where you just notice and allow the thoughts to be, without buying into them or trying to change them. I have four different metaphors for you to try out. I find these give us helpful visuals when a thought pops up.

1. Treat your unhelpful thoughts like an infomercial

Have you ever sat and watched bad day-time TV? Maybe you find yourself home sick from work, sprawled on the couch with a cup of tea and a hot water bottle, watching re-runs of a cheesy reality TV show. Mid-show, right before you get to the juicy bit and find out whether Brad gets that rose, an infomercial pops up. There's a lot of talk about there being 'three easy payments', and you watch a tanned woman with gravity-defying hair selling a product like some ridiculous machine that is supposed to 'shake the fat right off you' (good lord, how hard is this thing shaking?!) or some can opener that automatically spins the lid right off the can and turns it into an origami crane (okay, that's definitely not a thing). Either way, you do one of three things in this moment: you turn off the TV/turn down the volume, you change channels to find something else to listen to, or you tune out entirely, pivoting your attention to your cup of tea or taking a bathroom break.

What's happening here? You know that infomercials are useless and that it doesn't benefit you in any way to pay attention to them. So, you let them fade into the background and you switch your focus. You most certainly don't buy the product. (Okay, yes, there was that one time you bought that split-end-cutting hair brush that broke the second time you used it and we don't talk about that any more . . . but mostly you don't buy the product!)

You can respond to your unhelpful or inner critic thoughts in the same way you respond to these infomercials. You know they are trying to peddle ideas that you don't need or want. So you notice them for what they are and then tune out, pivoting your attention and not buying into the thought.

2. Treat your unhelpful thoughts like spam emails

When you get sent an email from some website you can't remember subscribing to, or from a person claiming you've won the lotto and all you need to do is reply with  your credit card details, you send the email to your spam folder. You delete it. You certainly don't read into it or engage in a conversation with the sender.

You can treat your unhelpful thoughts like this, too. When they pop up in your inbox (i.e. your mind), you can notice them, label them for what they are — 'Okay, this is a spam thought!' — and then direct those thoughts to the spam folder in your mind by not giving them the time, focus or attention they want. Unsubscribe! After you redirect to spam or unsubscribe from these thoughts enough times, they will eventually stop appearing in your inbox entirely.

3. Treat your unhelpful thoughts like books in a library

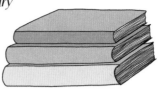

You go to the library looking for a book on caring for indoor plants (because you lost control a bit and now you have 20, and the maidenhair fern is looking particularly angry). As you run your finger along the spines of the books on the shelf, you notice all sorts of titles: *Excel Spreadsheets for Dummies, Paleo Cooking on a Budget, Hairstyles of the 1970s* . . . the list goes on. Do you pull them out of the shelf and start reading? Do you check these books out of the library? No. They're not what you're looking for, they're not interesting to you and you know you don't have to read them all.

Treat your thoughts a bit like books in a library. Just because they're there and maybe they catch your attention for a second, this does not mean you need to check them out and read them. You can leave unhelpful thoughts on the shelf.

> Treat your thoughts a bit like books in a library. Just because they're there and maybe they catch your attention for a second, this does not mean you need to check them out and read them.

4. Treat your unhelpful thoughts like 'that person' in your life (possibly my favourite)

Right now, bring to mind someone in your life that irks you. Maybe they're someone you just tolerate. Or you find yourself desperately trying not to roll your eyes when they talk. You know for sure you wouldn't go to this person for advice because you don't value their opinion. I'm sure we all have someone like this in our lives, or we have had them in the past. It might be your slightly creepy great-uncle Ted, your old boss Marlene — who definitely had no idea what she was doing — or your annoying neighbour Carl, who is just a downright pest. Now you name your inner critic after this person.

When those unhelpful thoughts pop into your mind, you can give them the full, unfiltered eye-roll, topped off with a confident 'That's old Marlene talking again. I don't need to take this on board.' (P.S. I've personally named my inner critic Patricia, and she can be a right persistent pain in the ass at times.)

With any of these approaches; I find they work best when combined with equal lashings of self-compassion and humour. It's okay to be kind to yourself, and to have a little giggle along the way.

Summary

- Your thoughts, actions and emotions are all interconnected. While you can't directly change your emotions, you can change your behaviours and the way you respond to your thoughts in order to influence your feelings.

- Look out for unhelpful thinking styles and learn to name them.

- Practise challenging your unhelpful thoughts with logic, fact, balance and compassion.

- There are certain conditions that make your brain more 'sticky' and vulnerable. Have compassion for yourself during these times, and take your 'sticky thoughts' with a grain of salt.

- Remember that thoughts are not facts. Don't believe everything you think — approach some thoughts like spam emails and send them straight to the junk folder in your brain!

RE-WRITE YOUR LIMITING BELIEFS

Underneath the layer of conscious thought and unhelpful thinking styles lie our core and limiting beliefs. Often operating at a subconscious level, these deeply ingrained narratives frequently go unobserved and unchallenged. Until now! Not everything you believe is true, so get out your pencil because it's time to re-write the scripts that are holding you back.

Core Beliefs

A core belief is a strongly held view of yourself, other people or the world. Sometimes they are helpful and true, like if you believe 'I am a worthy person' or 'most people have good intentions'. Sometimes they are unhelpful, no longer serving us — these are your limiting beliefs.

Here are some commonly held limiting beliefs. See if any of these pop out and bop you in the nose (i.e. resonate with you as something you believe):

- 'I'm not good enough.'
- 'I'm unlovable.'
- 'I'm a failure.'
- 'People are going to reject me/leave me.'
- 'I can never stick to anything.'
- 'People can't be trusted.'
- 'The world is a scary/ dangerous place.'
- 'I can't make friends.'
- 'I'm a loser.'
- 'Bad things always happen to me.'
- 'I'm stupid.'
- 'Everyone else is better than/more worthy than me.'
- 'I can't change.'
- 'Other people's needs are more important than mine.'
- 'I'll always be alone.'
- 'I can't do it.'
- 'I'm not smart enough.'
- 'I always fall for the wrong people.'
- 'I won't be happy until I have X amount of money/meet someone/get that job.'

Core beliefs sometimes come to exist through our strongly internalised inner critics whispering the same old stories in our ears over time. They also come to be when we gather together a whole suitcase of traumatic, painful and significant events in our lives and create a story out of what all of these things mean.

Sometimes we fiercely hold on to and believe things that just aren't true. Here's an example (if you still believe in the Tooth Fairy and Santa, you must avert your eyes immediately and skip ahead to the next page!).

Once upon a time, you believed with your whole heart in the Tooth Fairy. You believed in Santa. You believed in a number of mythical and wondrous fictional characters.

For years, you just knew that when you lost a tooth you should place it under your pillow at night when you went to bed. A fairy would fly into your room while you slept, take your tooth (what on earth did she do with them all?!) and place a shiny gold coin in its place. Every Christmas Eve, you believed that a jolly man with rosy cheeks and a jiggly belly somehow squeezed himself down the chimney (through your heat pump vents, even) and placed presents at the bottom of the Christmas tree. Then, after a few years, you finally began to question these beliefs before realising that they weren't true. The things you fiercely believed for so long were made-up stories.

Were you a fool to believe these things? No! (And, quite frankly, they're delightful things to believe.) Not only were you told these characters were real, but you had evidence for their existence. Cold, hard evidence. In my household, Santa ate the cookies I left for him, he sometimes left snowy boot prints on the carpet — which, had I cared to investigate, I would have discovered were made from icing sugar — and the Tooth Fairy once left me a letter (it didn't occur to me that it was odd that the Tooth Fairy and my mum had the exact same handwriting).

The last time I made this analogy to a group of women I was coaching, one of the participants said, 'Yes! I even saw Santa with my own eyes!' Some of our parents would go to the effort of dressing up in costumes — the Easter Bunny, elves, all sorts of things. How could we not believe the stories were true?!

Let me help explain core beliefs further by using another example. Let's bring back Jane (for more on Jane, see pages 118–129).

Jane held the limiting beliefs 'I am not good enough' and 'people are going to reject me/leave me'. These beliefs sat underneath everything Jane did, informing her decisions, interfering with her interactions with others (especially

Naomi) and halting her confidence in trying new things and putting herself out there.

In order to discover where this limiting core belief came from, Jane and I constructed a 'life map'. We drew out a timeline from birth right through to the present and, along that timeline, we plotted events in her life where she had come to the conclusion 'I am not good enough' or where someone had rejected or left her. Jane's life map looked something like this:

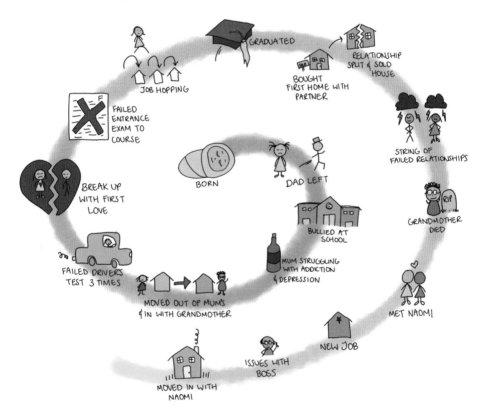

Jane believed she wasn't good enough because she had a lifetime of situations that seemed to prove it. She believed that people were going to reject her after drawing that conclusion based on people leaving in her life.

Limiting core beliefs are a bit like the 'rose-tinted glasses' you wear early on in a new relationship; only these glasses are grey-tinted and make everything look dull, negative and biased towards an unflattering view of yourself, people or the world. What's that about, you ask? It's called 'confirmation bias', and it explains our tendency to seek out evidence to support and confirm the things that we already believe. For example, if you believe 'people always leave me', your confirmation bias might have you subconsciously seeking out relationships with the wrong people, which inevitably end up not working out and thus confirming your belief. It may also lead you to forming friendships with people struggling with the same fears and issues; you all get together and talk about 'useless partners who always leave' and how 'you can't trust anyone' and further add to your pile of evidence. In order to prove your own beliefs, you may also act in ways that seek out certain reactions in others — pushing people away and testing limits until you sabotage your own relationships, exclaiming afterwards, 'See?! Everyone always leaves!'

These beliefs, whether we are aware of them or not, are always operating at a subconscious level. They steer our views, behaviours, relationships and choices. And when we come to realise that they no longer serve us, we can take steps towards letting them go and re-writing them. Here are some steps you can take to do this.

- **Step 1:** Identify your limiting core beliefs. This can be tricky, especially as they often sit outside of your conscious awareness. You might have an idea of what yours are simply by reading through the list of common limiting beliefs mentioned previously. You could also use what I call the 'drill-down method'. Here's how this works. First, start off with a harsh thought or inner critic statement, then ask yourself, 'If this is true, what does that say about me?' Your answer might be the limiting core belief. If not, ask again of your answer, 'If this is true, what does that say about me?'

  Let's go back to one of Jane's thoughts to try out the drill-down method. Jane thought, 'I should just end the relationship. Nothing ever works for me, anyway.' Jane would ask herself 'If it is true that nothing ever works for me, what does that say about me?' She might say, 'Well, it means that I am terrible in relationships.' Jane could drill down further here 'If it is true that I am terrible in relationships, what does that say about me?' She might answer, 'That I'm destined to end up single and alone.' Then Jane could drill down even further if she wanted to 'If it is true that I'm destined to end up single and alone, what does that say about me?' Jane might conclude 'Everyone always leaves me.' Or, 'I'm not good enough.' Now she has got to the heart of the matter; she has found her core limiting belief.

- **Step 2:** Acknowledge when a core belief has been triggered or might be informing a thought or behaviour. Jane realised that her core belief was being triggered when her partner did things like not contacting her in the day. Naomi was unable to call or text Jane at work because she couldn't have her phone on her. Her job demanded her full attention, and this had nothing to do with her love or commitment for Jane. When Jane responded with passive-aggression or the silent treatment, this behaviour was informed by the trigger of her limiting belief.

- **Step 3:** Call out the belief at play: 'This is a limiting belief of mine. It is not true. It no longer serves me.'

- **Step 4:** Understand the things that have contributed to the formation of this belief. You could create a life map, like Jane did.

- **Step 5:** Figure out what has been maintaining this belief. Are there relationships in your life right now that are unhealthy or play into you believing this? Is it simply that you didn't know about it? Has there been self-sabotaging getting in the way of you making changes? Are you engaging in behaviours to confirm your beliefs? Jane's belief was being maintained because she wasn't aware of it, yet it was being triggered frequently in her relationship with Naomi. Not only this, but when Jane responded to Naomi with the silent treatment, this was frustrating and hurtful for Naomi. Sometimes, as a result, Naomi would snap at Jane — or walk out and sleep the night at a friend's place. Jane would then use this response as further evidence to support her limiting belief, not realising its part to play in this cycle occurring in the first place.

- **Step 6:** Build evidence for all the things in your life that don't support this belief. These things will support a new, more healthy and helpful core belief. Think about all the things that have happened that you have dismissed, ignored or downplayed (unconsciously or not) because they disprove this limiting belief. To do this, Jane and I added to her life map. We included all the things we could think of, big and small, that did NOT support her belief 'I'm not good enough and people always leave', and instead supported the beliefs 'I am good enough', 'people can be trusted' and 'people come and go and this doesn't reflect on my worth'. This was the more realistic reflection of her life, but Jane had blinkers on and was dismissing all of these things.

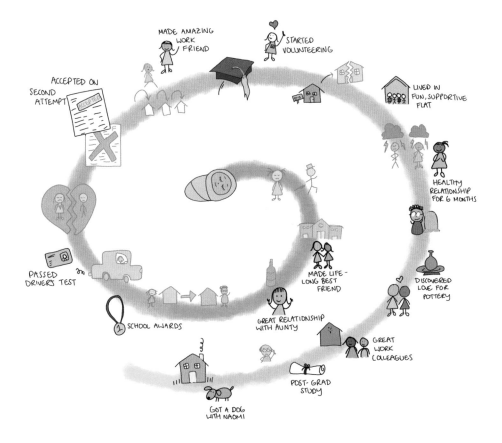

As humans, we like to view our world through a filter; we look for things that fit in with or support the beliefs we already have, and we set aside the things that don't. Acknowledging all of the events that support a healthy core belief is an important step in the deconstruction of the limiting one.

Step 7: Begin to act in ways that support the formation of your new, healthy core belief. Remember the CBT triangle from page 116? We know that we can start to act differently, changing our behaviours, and that this will flow on and affect our thoughts/beliefs and our emotions. So, you can actually be acting in healthy ways before you necessarily even believe that you deserve to or before your new core belief is integrated. Often, action needs to come before the belief does. Through our actions, we build evidence and, most importantly, we show up for ourselves. A question I love to ask is, 'How would you act if you did believe [insert healthy belief here]?' For Jane, this might be: 'How would I act if I did believe that I was good enough?' Here is what she might do.

Step 8: Continue to catch moments where your thoughts/ actions are in response to your old belief and adjust accordingly. Something to be aware of when you're working on these old narratives and limiting core beliefs is the 'self-fulfilling prophecy'. When you have a strongly held belief, this influences the way you think, what you expect to happen and your actions. Say you have the belief 'I never stick to anything' or 'I'm a failure', and then you go and start a new hobby — your belief is going to show up in that. You'll think, 'This is too hard. I'm not understanding this right away. Maybe I don't like this. I should just quit before I'm in too deep.' As a result, you don't show up to all of the classes, you put in less effort, you might drop out entirely. And this then confirms the original belief of 'I never stick to anything' and 'I'm a failure' — a self-fulfilling prophecy. The same thing happens when we flip the limiting belief to a positive one. Say you believe, 'I can make changes in my life'. You might put in the effort it takes to make those changes. You might fail but use that as a learning curve and continue to practise and persevere. Your persistence turns into competence, and this confirms your belief that you are able to make changes in your life.

Remember this: the traumas and things that happened to you (that contributed to the formation of these beliefs) were not your fault. However, they are now your responsibility to heal from. Take back your power.

New Beliefs

I want to start here by giving you a couple of simple reminders to guide you in your journey to letting go of limiting beliefs. It's time to step into healthy beliefs that affirm your self-worth and self-love. Remember:

> Build trust in yourself by showing up for yourself.
>
> Actions build evidence.
> Evidence builds belief.

You can begin to act in ways that support self-love and a belief in yourself before you actually believe those things. It's normal to fall back into old habits and old ways of thinking, and to be pulled into playing out old beliefs and scripts. Hold compassion for yourself as you step into authoring your own story with intention, healing and self-love.

If you find yourself actively rejecting a new belief because it sits so far outside of what you currently think, then re-write the new belief to feel a little more realistic for right now. This might look like putting the starter 'I am working on believing that . . .' in front of it. It might mean re-writing it entirely. We are trying not to create too much resistance and cognitive dissonance (for more on that, see page 28). Sometimes if you flip 180 on a belief it just doesn't feel realistic or believable, so aim for a 90-degree shift instead! For instance, instead of moving from 'people are going to reject me' to

Repetition is key — you need to act in ways that reject old beliefs and support new ones over and over again.

'all people are trustworthy and love me' (which you probably won't believe!), try moving to this: 'People come and go for many reasons. This does not define my worth. I trust that the right people will come into my life and accept me for who I am.'

Repetition is key — you need to act in ways that reject old beliefs and support new ones over and over again. Repeat new beliefs and actions intentionally and frequently.

Little things are big things. All the simple and small things that you might think don't matter or are insignificant add up to big things. When you say yes to overtime at work when you promised yourself you wouldn't, when you snooze your alarm for the eighth time after you told yourself you would get up early for yoga, when you cancel your plans for a massage because your friend wants you to help them, when you engage in a gossip session at work just to fit in — even though it makes you feel uncomfortable . . . all of these 'small things' are micro-abandonments of self that add up to an overall lack of self-trust and self-worth. Pay attention to these little things, and the big things (like beliefs) will begin to fall into place too.

And finally, cut yourself some slack. You're allowed to have days where you feel like a bag of potatoes. You're allowed to have times when you don't work on your goals. You're allowed to have moments of self-doubt, of fear, of wanting to crawl into PJs for a week! You are human. No one has unfaltering self-belief at all times,

and no one floats around on a cloud of constant inner peace. All
of this work is not about arriving at some destination of utopia.
The journey is the destination. And the mess and the chaos, when
combined with compassion and grace, is the goal.

And finally, cut yourself some slack.
You're allowed to have days where
you feel like a bag of potatoes.

Summary

- Core limiting beliefs develop over the years as we link up our negative life experiences or traumas and attribute a story or meaning to those things.

- These beliefs hold us back and don't take into account the full story — often they are downright untrue.

- We can re-write our beliefs by beginning to break down evidence for our old beliefs while working to build evidence to support new ones.

- It's important to build self-trust and new beliefs through action. We can act in ways that support healthy narratives even before we necessarily believe them.

- You are the author of your own story.

LET GO OF WHAT OTHERS THINK

When you get caught up in worrying about what other people think, or in comparing yourself to others, you outsource your sense of self-worth. So, how can you let go of mind-reading and comparison and cut yourself some slack? Read on, you're about to find out!

Mind Reading

Back on pages 122–126, we learnt about unhelpful thinking styles; mind reading was one of these. Let's dive a little deeper into this particular pesky thought trap. Mind reading, like comparison, has deep roots in our biology. It's normal to try to gauge what others might be thinking; it used to matter greatly to our survival, because if your fellow cave-people thought you were a bit of a twit you might just find yourself kicked out of the tribe!

Mind reading is also a common sinkhole you might fall into if you are someone who experiences a lot of anxiety (especially social anxiety) or if you are a people-pleaser. Where this can all get a bit sticky is when you find yourself worrying often about what others think of you, caught up in spirals of fear of upsetting someone else or of not fitting in. It's exhausting, to say the least, when you become preoccupied by imagining you know what others think about you or living in fear of the judgement of others.

Case study

In one of my coaching groups, a lovely client called Lou discovered that her most frequent unhelpful thinking style was mind reading. She described work as the hardest environment to be in; every time a colleague seemed irritated or annoyed, she would automatically assume it was somehow about her. She was convinced that she must have done something wrong and their mood was her fault (this is also called personalisation). Lou would go into people-pleasing mode, feeling she needed to fix everything — which made her feel anxious and drained. Lou was constantly putting aside her own needs and feelings in order to focus her energy on others. All of this meant she found it almost impossible to say no to people. This spiral of people-pleasing and poor boundaries stemmed from her thinking that it was her fault how others felt.

As you can imagine, Lou was constantly on edge, always trying to read people's minds to gauge how she was being received by others. This not only made work an anxiety-ridden place to be, but also made it difficult to make new friends and show up as her authentic self with people. Lou's work was to:

Look out for those mind-reading thinking styles — when she noticed someone seemed annoyed and she was thinking 'This is about me!,' she had to catch that thought.

Watch out for personalisation. Lou made other people's reactions and emotions all about her, thinking she was somehow at fault or responsible. Other people are responsible for their own reactions and feelings.

Get clear on her boundaries and stick to them — when fears of upsetting others popped up, she was to acknowledge that but continue to hold the boundary. Lou knew it would feel uncomfortable at first and that she might experience some guilt, and that she needed to lean in to that. It was worth it for the long-term boost in self-worth.

Adopt a coping statement for herself: 'I do not know what other people are thinking. I am not responsible for what others feel. This is my "people-pleaser" coming up. I can sit with this discomfort.'

Test the validity of the unhelpful thought. If you think people are irritated at you (mind reading), you can check that out with them: 'Hey, I'm noticing you seem a bit off today. Is everything okay?' Lou might find out they are tired or struggling with something in their personal life, and then see that it isn't related to her. And if it was about her, she could either work to rectify that or hold her boundary and sit with the discomfort.

Challenge her rule 'I can't say no to people' — that was Lou's limiting belief talking. You can say no. It will take practice and it might feel icky at first. But you can do it.

Mind reading gets us into all kinds of trouble with ourselves and in our relationships. When we imagine we know what others are thinking, it tends to leave us internally stewing, feeling anxious and insecure.

On the flip side of mind reading, sometimes we project outwardly on to others. You might feel that certain people in your life should 'just know' how you feel or what you need. We tend to do this in our close and intimate relationships. Does any of this sound familiar?

- 'He should know I'm upset! It's obvious. Why isn't he comforting me?!'

- 'She should know by now I hate it when she's late.'

- 'They should have done the washing while I was out.'

- 'He should know it hurts me when he speaks to me like that.'

In these examples, unless it was explicitly stated to the other party, they may just not know. We know, yes — and because we know, we assume that others do, too.

How should you approach mind reading?

So, what do you do when you notice you are mind reading? First, cut yourself some slack and remember that this is a normal thinking style. You're not alone, and there is likely evolutionary reasons combined with life experiences that have brought about this way of thinking. But, as we have learnt, thoughts are just thoughts — not facts — and now you know about your mind reading tendencies, you can do something about it! Here are some ways to approach mind reading.

- Name it. Call it out. 'Oh, I'm mind reading here!'

- Have a mantra, like Lou's: 'This is mind reading. I don't know for sure what others are thinking.' Or 'others cannot read my mind', 'I am not responsible for fixing other people's feelings', 'it is my responsibility to state my needs to others', 'I cannot read people's minds — most people are far more worried about themselves than they are about me' or 'people are not judging me as harshly as I am judging myself — I can cut myself some slack'.

- Test the validity of the thought. This one takes a bit of courage, but you can actually take your thought and check it out with people. When we are mind reading, we are often thinking in extremes or being particularly hard on ourselves. Often when we test the thought out with someone, we find it either isn't true at all or that we were blowing it out of proportion. If you know the person well, you might be able to be super-honest: 'Hey, I get stuck on this idea that when people seem distracted they are actually mad at me. Is this how you are feeling?' Or: 'You seem a little off today — is everything okay?'

- Stick to your boundaries and your values, even when you are imagining that others are displeased with this. Trying to appease everyone by modifying your behaviour or tip-toeing around on eggshells trying to please others is a sure-fire way to burnout or feelings of anxiety and resentment. If you know that you really want A but you do B to keep someone else happy, you will always end up feeling let down and out of alignment.

- Be your true self, not a modified version because you think that's what others want. When you get caught up reading other people's minds, worrying what they think and adjusting all your behaviours based on your perception of what others want you to be, you are not living in alignment with who you really are. You may have been doing this for years and wonder, 'Who even am I?!' That's okay. It will take practice to get back to trusting who you are, what you really want and staying true to your needs. Ultimately, what this leads to is real and authentic relationships. Many people worry that if they stop living a life of people-pleasing they will lose people. The honest truth is that it is possible some relationships may be affected or even end — but this is the ending of a relationship that was based on you not having your needs met or being your true self, which is probably far more damaging and painful in the long run than the short-term pain of the relationship ending. What is more likely to happen with most relationships when you stop people-pleasing, is that they may go through an adjustment period while you both get used to your new boundaries, and then those who truly love and value you will stay. And I don't know about you, but those are the people I want in my life — true, real, reciprocal relationships.

- Practise sitting with the discomfort of not truly knowing what others are thinking all the time.

- Remember that you cannot control what other people think or feel. You are not responsible for others' feelings. It is not your job to fix them or modify your needs to appease others. Focus on what is in your control — your own thoughts and actions.

- Challenge your thoughts; be realistic and balanced. For example, 'He hasn't replied to my message, so he must be upset with me' becomes, 'He hasn't replied to my message. There could be any number of reasons for that. I can check that out later, and instead of waiting for him to reply, I can carry on with my day.'

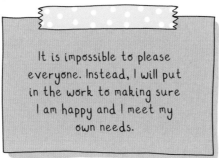

It is impossible to please everyone. Instead, I will put in the work to making sure I am happy and I meet my own needs.

A final thought that helps me snap out of mind reading . . . Next time you are mind reading, remember this: it's none of your business! What other people think and believe, quite frankly, is not our business. We can't waste our days trying to live our lives outside of ourselves in someone else's body. Come back home to you.

Comparison

Comparing yourself with others is a natural human behaviour, but does it help you to live your best life? Let's start delving into this by filling in this checklist. Have you ever . . .

☐ Found yourself scrolling mindlessly on social media and wishing you had what someone else has — their 'perfect skin', their body, their house, their family, their job, and so on?

☐ Felt envious of someone else at work because of their position, power or salary?

☐ Looked at a group photo and found your eyes pulled instantly to yourself to scrutinise and compare with others in the picture or nitpick at your hair, body and clothes?

☐ Had a 'friend' on social media who you don't really have contact with but whose life you follow and stories you watch because they seem like they 'have it all together' and you just can't seem to look away?

Try this instead:

> The next time I look at a photo of myself, I vow to pick out 3 things I love and am grateful for about myself, rather than instantly look for things I perceive as flaws.

Did you know there is actually an evolutionary and biological reason as to why we compare ourselves with others? That's right; it's actually encoded within us to engage in this behaviour. Let me explain. Travel back in time with me now, to cavemen days . . .

Imagine yourself, with your animal-skin dress and a bone through your hair. You're with your tribe of other cave-people, and everyone has their important jobs: foraging for berries, hunting, tending to the children or stoking the fire. It was absolutely crucial for your survival that you belonged to this tribe, that you fitted in and that others accepted you. And belonging also meant a chance for procreation — a primitive urge!

If you weren't accepted, you ran the risk of being an outcast. And if you were to be shunned from your group, you likely wouldn't survive

(what with all the sabre-toothed tigers around and so on). So, for this reason, you had to become aware of how you fit in and how you were being received by others around you. And that meant comparison. You compared your behaviour with theirs, you compared how well you were foraging, how well you were attracting mates and how well others responded to you. If, during your comparison, you noticed others were 'doing it better' or you were falling short of the mark, you were able to adjust your behaviour in order to remain in the tribe.

Fast-forward to today, and while so much has evolved, many of the primitive survival structures of our brains still remain. Nowadays our survival doesn't hinge so heavily on our tribes — we can pop to the local supermarket for berries and meat, swipe right on our phone to find a love match, and most of us have a heat pump rather than a pile of sticks and a couple of stones to rub together for fire. But, despite no longer relying on tribes for our survival, some of our caveman instincts remain. Like the comparison behaviour. Only now we compare our car with our neighbour's, we compare our weight with the women we see in beauty campaigns, we compare our jobs with our college classmates, we compare our parenting abilities with the image we are presented by friends on Facebook and we compare our day-to-day lives with the 'highlight reels' of strangers on social media. Rather than this comparison driving our behaviours for acceptance, it drives our sense of not being 'enough'. And this drives our feelings of guilt, shame, unworthiness and even anxiety and depression.

Companies and marketing teams know exactly how to work this 'comparison trait' to their advantage. I recently conducted an experiment on my own social media feed; I scrolled for ten minutes on Facebook and took note of all the ads I saw with an agenda to make me compare myself with someone else or feel 'less than' for the purpose of selling a product. In that time I saw: an ad for a weight-loss programme to fix my belly fat; a product that was supposed to make my hair shiny and strong; a marketing campaign of a woman who makes a five-figure salary every month, saying I should be able to, too; and an ad for a 'chin yoga' class to reduce my double chin (I felt personally attacked by that one!). We are bombarded by messages every day that we aren't good enough the way we are, or that we could be better, with the underlying promise that buying what they're selling will make us happy.

We know that comparison is a normal thing, so the first step for all you self-confessed comparison addicts out there is to give yourself some compassion and cut yourself some slack. There's a reason we do it; and now we understand our biology a little better, we can navigate around this and create some new habits. So, how do we stop the 'comparison game'? I have some ideas for you . . .

Try a social media cleanse. There are three ways to do this:

1. Scroll through your Instagram or Facebook feed and take note of any posts that bring up a sense of feeling 'less than'. If you catch yourself making comparisons between yourself and what you are seeing in a post, and that is making you feel crappy, you are going to unfollow the account that posts that content. For ads, you are going to click the three little dots at the top and select 'Hide ad'. The social media cleanse includes those 'guilty pleasure' accounts you follow, like the diet and exercise pages that you swear you're going to get around to, but don't,

and so you feel guilty every time they pop up. Or the healthy cooking page that you are so keen to try recipes from, but you are far too busy right now. (You always feel like the people who cook like that must be so much more organised and together than you.) Or the old acquaintance from high school who seems to always be radiating sunshine and drinking coffee by the beach. (You never speak, but you always compare your life with theirs.)

Case study

Many years ago I was working with a client; let's call her Zara. Zara was young, surrounded by friends, well-liked, beautiful, and crippled by self-doubt and insecurities. Among the many discussions and tools we explored in our work together was the impact of social media in her life. I challenged Zara to do a social media cleanse and to be honest and ruthless about it. Zara returned the next week to report that of the 1500 accounts that she followed on Instagram, she had deleted 900 of them. That means that 60 per cent of the content Zara was consuming every time she scrolled on her phone was making her feel unworthy, jealous or insecure. You can imagine the impact that this was having on her overall sense of worth and mental health.

2. Limit your time on certain apps. Most phones have a setting that can send you a notification when you have exceeded a set daily screen-time or app-use limit. You can evaluate your screen time and set boundaries for yourself. One hack you can try is moving your social media apps off your main

screen and into a folder — this breaks our thumb's naughty little unconscious habit of opening the apps and scrolling mindlessly through sheer boredom or as a coping strategy when we don't feel so good.

3. Take a screen-time or social-media detox. You can either delete certain apps for a period of time or stay off your phone entirely. Some people like to delete social media during the week, and reinstall it on weekends. You'll be surprised the shifts that occur when you take a few days' break from social media scrolling.

- Call out comparison when you catch yourself doing it. Notice when you are comparing yourself to others and name that.

- Compare yourself in a helpful way. You can do this by comparing yourself with someone who you admire and look up to who is also doing things that are accessible and achievable to you. Use them as inspiration and motivation, not as an impossible benchmark or a reason to beat yourself up.

- Compare yourself with yesterday's you or last year's you, and celebrate your achievements and the gains you have made. Then think about where you'd like to be in six months or a year from now, and make moves in that direction. A little note on this, though: you don't always have to be striving and improving. Good lord, it is OKAY to coast, to go backwards sometimes, to just chill out on the self-development work now and then. Constantly trying to grow, change and progress is exhausting!

- Check your standards and be realistic. Sometimes we judge

ourselves and our performance against someone who is a pro; they've spent years refining their craft. It's like looking at an Olympic gymnast and being annoyed at yourself because you can't do a handstand. Have you spent years training? No? Then let it go. On a more 'normal' scale, this applies when you judge yourself against your peers. Like slamming your cooking blunders (because you bloody hate cooking) and comparing yourself with your friend who bakes every weekend and makes a roast every Monday night because they love it. Make sure your standards are realistic, fair, achievable and non-perfectionistic, and that your comparisons matter to you and your values. Not everyone is good at everything.

Here are some journal prompts for you to further unpack comparison:

- What are the areas in my life in which I find myself comparing myself with others?

- If I didn't compare myself with others, how might I act/conduct myself differently?

- In what ways does comparison hold me back?

- How would life be different if I didn't compare myself with others? (Get really specific here about what this might look like or mean for you.)

- How could I begin to use comparison in a healthier way?

Summary

- Many of us get caught up in 'mind reading' and worry about what others think. Remind yourself to focus on what is within your control and focus on your own business.

- Comparison is a normal human behaviour. When you notice this, try to redirect your comparison to something more helpful.

- Be mindful of who/what you compare yourself to. Not everything is as it appears (especially with social media).

PROTECT YOUR ENERGY

It's important to protect your energy and honour your unique traits and needs — explore how you can do this with healthy boundaries. We look at the traits of highly sensitive people, the gifts this brings and how important it is not to abandon yourself to please others.

Boundaries

A boundary is an invisible line that you draw between you and 'not you'. It's where you end and another person begins. It's the limits you set that separate your space, your needs, your energy, your emotions, your body, your things, your responsibilities and your time. Having healthy boundaries is key to healthy relationships and your own mental wellbeing.

Healthy boundaries are a key element in self-worth/esteem, avoiding burnout, good mental health, self-care and a strong sense of who you are. Boundaries are important across so many different areas of your life: physical, time, emotional, sexual, intellectual, financial, material . . . and then there are the boundaries with yourself — your personal boundaries. Boundaries fall somewhere along a continuum like this:

Porous ---------- flexible ---------- Rigid

When your boundaries are too porous, you often find yourself 'giving in': people-pleasing, putting your needs aside and putting the feelings and needs of others above your own. This tends to result in you getting burnt-out, feeling violated, depressed or resentful of others around you that are benefiting from your lack of boundaries. Porous boundaries can lead to an abandonment of self. And when your boundaries are porous with yourself, this leads to a lack of self-care, not showing up for yourself and difficulty in sticking to goals.

On the other end of the spectrum, when your boundaries are too rigid you tend to have your walls up, never compromising or letting others in. This can lead to disconnection and issues in your relationships. When your boundaries are more flexible, you are able to hold your ground while compromising or changing your boundaries to suit your needs and the choices you want to make for your relationships. In saying this, there are absolutely times where you NEED to have those rigid boundaries. You need to have areas of your life that are a 'hard no' or a 'hell yes', and nothing in between.

Let's do a little self-evaluation. Think about the following areas of your life and rate how satisfied you are with the boundaries you hold there. Rate each category out of one to ten, with ten being extremely happy/very healthy boundaries and one being extremely unhappy/unhealthy boundaries.

EXERCISE

Home
/10

Think about: division of chores/cooking among the people you live with, who comes into your space and when, and so on.

Work
/10

Think about: hours put in over and above your contracted hours, work taken on that isn't your responsibility, whether you take all your lunch breaks, whether you are contactable/work on weekends, whether your work aligns with your values and lifestyle needs, whether you take your allocated holiday leave and sick days, and so on.

Partner

/10

Think about: time spent together versus alone, communication styles/argument styles (the way you speak to one another), whether you stay true to your values and needs, whether you communicate your wants and needs, your physical needs and expectations, your privacy, whether you communicate dissatisfaction or discomfort, how you handle finances, emotional availability and support, whether you are able to express and discuss your views and opinions, how you feel about your sex life, and so on.

Children

/10

Think about: how much you do for them that they could be doing (or learning to do) for themselves, screen time, time with them/time away from them, behaviours allowed in the home, ways of communicating, and so on.

Family

/10

Think about: visits (e.g. showing up unannounced), money you lend when you don't really want to/that isn't repaid or repaid on time, your family role (e.g. the family peacekeeper or therapist), time spent together, your level of responsibility in the family, topics of conversation (e.g. unwanted comments on your appearance or parenting), and so on.

Think about: emotional sharing versus burdening (sometimes our friends use us or we use them as a place to vent and purge without checking in around this first), money you lend, your role in the friendship (e.g. are you always the rescuer or the 'therapist'? Is it a two-way street?), your comfort with the topics of conversation, the time you put in, and so on.

Think about: loans to people that you may not want (or be able to afford) to give, your own spending and control limits, whether you stick to your budget/ have a budget, whether you stick to savings, whether you stick to your shopping list (rather than impulse spending), whether you over-spend on certain things that are outside of your budget, whether you stay true to your values and goals around money, taking on new debt, putting your own financial needs first, how often you eat takeout, and so on.

And lastly, the most important area of all (because it encompasses so much of the above and more):

Think about: how much time you dedicate to self-care, what/who you allow in your life, how you spend your time and whether this aligns with your values/what is important to you in life, how you allow yourself to speak to yourself or about others (e.g. inner critic thoughts or gossiping about others), sticking to commitments you make to yourself, time spent engaging in unhealthy behaviours and coping strategies, the time you go to bed at night and wake up in the morning (and whether this serves you), taking care of your basic physical and foundational needs (brushing your teeth, showering, drinking water, exercising, eating well), the types of things you consume (what you eat and drink), how much time you spend on screens/devices/certain apps, how you honour your physical space (e.g. no TV in the bedroom, or keeping on top of laundry), and so on.

Now, let me introduce you to Elaine.

Case study

Elaine was one of my self-development coaching clients. She described herself as someone who 'gave it all'. She worked long hours in a corporate job, then spent her evenings cooking family meals, packing lunches for her adolescent children and managing the family home (e.g. laundry, cleaning, paying bills and all that thrilling business that soaks up our time as humans) before finally falling asleep, phone in hand and emails waiting. On the weekends, she did what her family wanted to do — shuttling the kids to sports, following along to the activities they loved (that she didn't), responding to work emails that pinged on her phone, cleaning the house . . . Elaine felt burnt-out and a little resentful. She was lacking in boundaries. Elaine needed much more rigid boundaries, as they were too porous:

- *Responding to work emails outside of hours.*
- *Making lunch every day when her children were capable of doing some (if not all) of this work themselves.*

- *Spending her time doing what everyone else wanted.*

- *Not having boundaries around her phone being used when she was trying to sleep.*

- *Not prioritising her own needs and self-care.*

Ultimately, Elaine was saying 'yes' to all of these things. Not in an outward 'oh yay, give me all the work to do' kind of way, but in a subtle 'not speaking my mind' way, where she was allowing the people in her life to demand more of her than she wanted to give. She was permissive in her burnout by going along with it. It was time for Elaine to state her needs and draw some lines in the sand.

My coaching clients often discover that the area they lack boundaries the most is with themselves. Did you find this, too? We often think of boundaries as things we need to have in place with other people. But are you showing up for you? Are you keeping promises to you? There are so many ways that we fail to turn up for ourselves. Do any of these sound familiar to you?

- You tell yourself you're going to get up early to go for a walk. You set your alarm, but come morning you hit the snooze button eleven times before finally getting up, late for work and berating yourself for being lazy.

- You tell yourself you need to be more mindful of money this month, but end up going for an unplanned spending spree on clothes or an online shopping rampage.

- You say you're going to start eating healthier foods, but you continue not to pack a lunch and grab takeaways on the go.

- You're stressed and overwhelmed. You know you need some down-time this weekend, but a friend needs you or work comes up and you end up spending hours on the weekend doing something you don't want to be doing, feeling resentful and more stressed.

- You continue to speak to yourself using harsh and judgemental language, even though you're trying so hard not to listen to your inner critic.

- You tell yourself you need an early night, but end up watching Netflix or scrolling on your phone until midnight.

- Your work is a major source of stress, but you check and respond to work emails outside of work hours and on weekends.

- Someone in your life is treating you badly, but you fail to stand up for yourself or speak up.

- You feel guilty if you take time out just for yourself.

- You keep saying yes to things that you really want to say no to.

- You keep getting sucked into the pointless arguments between two family members.

- You find yourself gossiping with a friend or coworkers when you know this isn't the type of energy you want to be around or involved with.

When it comes to setting new boundaries, there are some things that may be helpful to remember:

- The first person you need to convince of your new boundary is yourself. You need to know why you are doing it, why it matters, how you will set it, and how you will manage the possible pushback from the person/people you set the boundary with. You have to convince yourself first, so you will hold your ground.

- Saying no to something or someone also means you get to say yes — yes to yourself, yes to your needs, yes to your values and yes to your priorities.

- You are not responsible for how someone else reacts to your boundaries. Your job is to set the boundary. Their job is to manage their own reaction. If there is anger or hurt, that is okay, but it isn't your job to fix and it certainly doesn't warrant you giving in on your boundary.

- Yes, you may feel guilty when you set a boundary. That's a normal and natural response and will get easier in time. Sit with the discomfort. Hold the boundary. The long-term gain is worth the short-term pain.

Something that may also help you when setting boundaries is to shift from an 'external' or 'other-focused' boundary to an 'internal' or 'me-focused' boundary. Moving from 'I will not let you speak to me like that' to 'I remove myself from situations where there is yelling and disrespect'. Moving from 'if you cancel on me again, I will not be speaking to you any more' to 'I honour and protect the time and energy I put into my relationships'. Making this shift can help you feel more empowered, as you bring the focus back to yourself and what is within your control, rather than focusing on the behaviour of others and things outside of your control.

What Elaine realised was that much of the overwhelm and burnout she was feeling was a result of her porous boundaries, and that, empoweringly, much of this was within her control to change. She decided to leave work at work, becoming strict about not answering work emails in the evenings and on weekends. She tasked her children with making their own lunches, and she made conscious plans that included things she liked to do on weekends. The family set up a 'chores list' for the housework and Elaine took ten minutes to herself after work every day to have a cup of tea and take a breather.

HOLDING FIRM TO MY BOUNDARIES DOES NOT MAKE ME SELFISH, RUDE, DIFFICULT, AGGRESSIVE OR UNKIND. I AM ENTITLED TO MY NEEDS. I DESERVE TO BE RESPECTED & HEARD.

Why is setting boundaries so hard?

It's normal to have fears or trepidation when setting boundaries. You may be fearful that by setting the boundary you will be judged, or that you'll fail at sticking to it, or that you won't be able to cope with the discomfort and guilt that may arise. It's also scary to set a boundary because it means putting yourself and your needs out there; it can bring up a fear of rejection, getting hurt, not being seen or . . . being seen! You might be worried you'll get let down or you'll be disapproved of or that you will have to cope with conflict . . . there are so many things that can hold you back.

When you know what your fears are, you can plan accordingly and respond to them. And, importantly, you can continue to push ahead, out of your comfort zone, into your growth zone and make the changes you need to. Don't let your decisions be driven by fear.

Sometimes setting boundaries feels so unnatural or difficult because you were modelled unhealthy boundary-setting growing up. You may have been raised in a home where boundaries were greatly lacking or non-existent. Maybe you had a father who was a people-pleaser and never said no, a mother who struggled with anxiety or self-esteem and always put herself down and her needs on the back-burner, or parents who impinged on your boundaries and needs, putting their own above yours while you were expected to conform to their rule book.

> Sometimes setting boundaries feels so unnatural or difficult because you were modelled unhealthy boundary-setting growing up.

Other times, setting a boundary is hard because a belief about yourself is triggered or feels out of alignment. Something like 'I'm a kind and peaceful person, so I can't set boundaries', 'I don't do conflict', 'I just go with the flow', 'I'm too timid' or 'I can't let people down'. These views of yourself will need to be gently challenged. How well are these really working for you?

If you call yourself a 'people-pleaser', then setting boundaries might feel totally uncomfortable and out of character for you. You may have had years of putting others' needs above your own, so setting boundaries might be like learning a foreign language! People-pleasing is usually an abandonment of self. Essentially, you are saying:

> 'Other people's needs matter more than my own.'
>
> 'My worth is tied up in how I serve others or how others perceive me.'
>
> 'As long as others are happy, it doesn't matter how I feel.'
>
> 'I will abandon my own needs, wants, happiness and boundaries if that benefits others.'

Don't beat yourself up for this. People-pleasing is usually a behaviour that we learnt for good reason. Maybe it was a way to protect yourself and keep yourself safe initially, by keeping those around you appeased and on-side. Maybe it was a learnt behaviour, as you watched a parent model this as you grew up. It may even be a trauma response or a threat response, as discussed in chapter 2 about the fawn response. So, while this behaviour may have served a function initially, it is likely no longer serving you today.

A common fear in setting boundaries with people in your life is this: 'What if they don't like it and they leave?' A fear of judgement, rejection and getting hurt may be the very reason you struggle with boundaries in the first place, so the risk of these fears coming true by setting and reinforcing a boundary sounds like a very scary thing.

The truth is, when you set a boundary with someone there may be pushback against it. Suddenly the unspoken 'rules' in your relationship have changed and this may be hard for the other person to take. Ideally, everyone will come around, accepting and respecting the boundaries you set. And, in mutual and healthy relationships this is often the case. However, you do have to prepare yourself for the scenario where the other party does have a strong reaction to your new boundary. And yes, sometimes the person may not agree to or respect your new line in the sand.

In this instance, you have to decide on the consequence. There is a chance that the outcome is that this relationship changes completely, either ending or creating more distance between you. Here's the thing about that: if this person was only in your life because your lack of boundaries was serving them and you were being hurt in the process, is this the kind of person or relationship you really want in your life?

When you do let go of relationships that aren't serving you, or if these people move on from you because your values no longer align, this is creating space for people to come into your life who do align with you.

How do you set healthy boundaries?

Follow these four simple (but not always easy) steps.

1 — **Get clear on your boundaries**

First, you need to identify what your boundaries are and why they matter/why you need the boundary. Your boundaries need to be in line with your needs and values (the things that matter the most to you). You might start by thinking about areas or relationships in your life right now where you feel a sense of resentment, being taken for granted, or burnout. These are likely areas that require more boundaries from you. If you realise now that there are a lot of areas in your life that are lacking boundaries, start small. It's okay to test out the water with a couple of boundaries, or put in place a few test runs!

2 — **State your boundaries**

It's all well and good to be clear on what your boundaries are, but that means nothing unless you outwardly communicate these to others. Even though this may feel unnatural and uncomfortable, clearly state your needs and boundaries with those who need to hear them (and yes, this includes yourself!). Remember that the first person you need to convince of your boundaries is yourself, and that it is not your responsibility how others react to those boundaries. Another little tip here: don't over-explain. It isn't your job to convince the other person of your boundary; you do not need a novel-length excuse as to why you are setting this boundary. You also don't need to fill the boundary with apologies!

3 Hold strong

You might experience guilt or anxiety in setting your new boundary. That's okay! That's normal when you're doing something new and out of your comfort zone. Don't let these feelings of discomfort or the reaction of others sway you. Hold the line. And remember this: it is okay to re-evaluate your boundaries and for them to change over time. You might start hard and strong on a boundary at first, and then realise you are happy to ease up on this a little in time. That's cool.

4 Set consequences

Before you set the boundary, you will need to have some consequences in mind in the event that the person does not adhere to your boundary. AND you have to be willing to stick to those consequences! First and foremost, know this: the person may cross your boundary unintentionally at first, or without malice. This is a new 'rule' and they may just be trying to adjust to what this means. No one is perfect, so we have to be mindful of our expectations initially. You can restate and remind them, if the boundary is crossed. Hopefully this will be enough, but if it isn't you will need consequences. For instance:

- 'If you continue to bring up my weight at family functions, I will limit my attendance going forward/walk away from the conversation/leave early.'

- 'I can loan you this money, but it must be paid back by next Sunday. If it is not, I will not be lending you money again.'

- 'If I continue to be disrespected at work and asked to work outside of my contract, I will look for a new job.'

- 'If you show up late again, I won't be making another time to meet with you this month.'

- 'I expect XYZ from my partner in a romantic relationship. If we don't align on this, it is best that we go our separate ways.'

This language is obviously rather bland and direct. If this is the kind of bluntness you need, then go for it! Otherwise, you will of course find your own way to state and uphold your boundaries, using language that works for you.

How might others react when you set a boundary?

Okay, so you're thinking it's time to set that boundary but you want to prepare yourself for how others might react to you. Fair enough . . . here are some possibilities. They might:

- Respect it.
- Take some time to get used to it.
- Try to push back against it.
- Exit the relationship in one way or another.
- Change their behaviour to honour it.
- Try to guilt you.
- Remind you about the fact the behaviour used to be 'acceptable' (of course it probably wasn't to you, but you never voiced that).
- Demand you explain and justify it.

> **The best way to build boundaries with yourself is to start small and build up some trust in yourself.**

Prepare yourself for others' reactions — you've got this!

If the area you need boundaries with the most is with yourself, then expect reactions like 'falling off the bandwagon', reverting to old habits, finding it hard and clunky to stick to the commitments you make to yourself, and that pesky inner critic trying to talk you out of setting and sticking to boundaries in the first place. We know that our brains like the old and the familiar, so prepare for this. But keep showing up for you. The best way to build boundaries with yourself is to start small and build up some trust in yourself. Your brain needs to start collecting evidence that you can be trusted to follow through and to be there for you. So prove it to yourself.

To close out this section, I'll leave you with some points to ponder or journal on, and your basic rights. Consider these:

Reflecting on the different areas in my life, where do I most need to set boundaries?

What needs do I currently have that aren't being met? How could healthy boundaries help me with meeting those needs?

What has kept me from setting boundaries in the past? (Thoughts, beliefs, ideas about myself, fears, etc.)

What do I stand to gain from setting a boundary?

While you're thinking about the above points, remember your basic rights:

MY BASIC RIGHTS

I have the right to...
- have my needs met & respected
- feel safe in relationships
- be treated with respect
- say 'no'
- change my mind
- make mistakes
- feel my emotions
- express my opinions
- set my own priorities
- set limits
- be assertive
- walk away from toxic or unhealthy relationships

Highly Sensitive People

Looking back on my life, if I had a dollar for every time I was called 'sensitive', was told to 'harden up' or that I needed 'thicker skin' to make it in the world . . . I would have enough money to buy some decent noise-cancelling ear muffs to help drown out all that racket! If you're anything like me, you need decompression time after being around people. And I have ruined more tops than I can count by ripping the tag off in a frenzy because I couldn't stand the feeling of it scratching my neck for one second longer.

Maybe you can relate? You might be someone who is desperate to get home and put on snuggly pants and fuzzy socks after being at a loud bar for 30 minutes. You might feel worn out and depleted after being around people or loud environments. Maybe you're the kind of person who cries in arguments easily and you question if you're strong enough.

Research suggests that somewhere around 30 per cent of people are 'highly sensitive people' (or HSPs), so there's every chance that either you are one or you know one!

What is a highly sensitive person?

First off, it is not a diagnosis and it isn't a disorder. It is a set of character/personality traits. Basically, as an HSP, your brain is geared to be more sensitive and responsive to stimuli around you. You probably process information more thoroughly, are more reactive to certain things, and maybe you take in sensory information differently than others.

Your brain actually responds more strongly to social and emotional cues than the brains of your less sensitive colleagues and friends.

If we scanned the brain of an HSP and the brain of someone 'less sensitive' while the two were viewing a photo of someone looking upset, you would see far more blood-flow and activity in the areas involved in emotion recognition and awareness in the HSP's brain.

Humans have something called a 'mirror neuron system', which is basically where parts of our brains will light up in response to someone else, mimicking and mirroring what this person is displaying. Put simply, if I sat in a chair opposite you and cried, your brain would light up the same areas as if you were crying. You might start to feel sad.

HSPs are highly attuned to the emotions of others, and this is a trait that is often referred to as being an 'empath'. Here's a little empath quiz to see for yourself:

- ☐ Are you highly aware of the emotions of others around you?
- ☐ Do you sometimes feel those emotions yourself?
- ☐ Are you particularly aware of the needs of others?
- ☐ Do you get overwhelmed by crowds?
- ☐ Do people trust you with their problems?
- ☐ Do you care deeply about other people, animals and the world?
- ☐ Do you dislike or avoid conflict?
- ☐ Do you sometimes struggle with boundaries or saying no?
- ☐ Do people go to you for a listening ear?
- ☐ Do you work hard to make others happy?

How many answers did you respond to with a 'yes'? If it was more than half, you might just be an empath!

What are the common traits of highly sensitive people?

Do you identify with many of the things on this list?

- ☐ You can become exhausted by 'absorbing' the emotions of people around you.
- ☐ You can be jumpy, getting frights easily.
- ☐ You get sensory overload by strong smells, loud noises, intense lights and some fabrics touching your skin.
- ☐ You feel the need to withdraw for quiet alone time after a busy day or event.
- ☐ You may avoid situations that you know are going to be overwhelming or highly sensory.
- ☐ You feel things deeply.
- ☐ You can be easily rattled by time pressure of having a lot on your to-do list.
- ☐ You are extremely affected by witnessing/hearing of neglect, cruelty, abuse and violence.
- ☐ You've been called 'low maintenance' (probably because you're either busy putting the needs of others before your own, or because you are able to read the needs of others).
- ☐ You can struggle to make decisions.
- ☐ Sometimes change is quite hard for you.

Looking at that list, or knowing first-hand for yourself what it's like to be an HSP, you might be thinking, 'This is a curse!' You're probably acutely aware of the challenges . . .

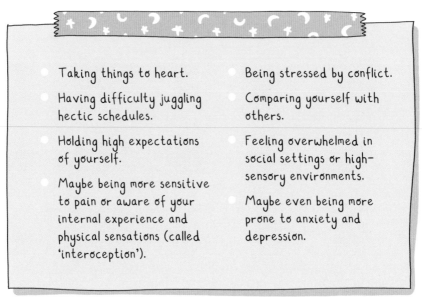

- Taking things to heart.
- Having difficulty juggling hectic schedules.
- Holding high expectations of yourself.
- Maybe being more sensitive to pain or aware of your internal experience and physical sensations (called 'interoception').
- Being stressed by conflict.
- Comparing yourself with others.
- Feeling overwhelmed in social settings or high-sensory environments.
- Maybe even being more prone to anxiety and depression.

BUT I am here to tell you it is not all doom and gloom. In fact, being an empath or an HSP is a gift. Why?

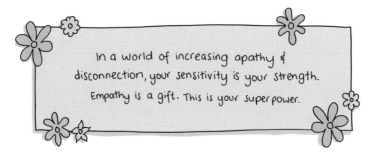

In a world of increasing apathy & disconnection, your sensitivity is your strength. Empathy is a gift. This is your superpower.

Good things about being an HSP

You feel sensations and emotions deeply.

You notice things others don't.

You're empathetic — your brain literally lights up and mirrors what you see!

You're passionate.

You make a great leader or entrepreneur.

You're innovative.

You are intuitive.

You're considerate.

You're detail-oriented.

You relish positive emotions.

You're often creative.

You can be a deep thinker.

You're reflective.

You understand others' emotions.

You're a good judge of character.

You have close, meaningful relationships with others.

You can pick out subtle changes in your environment or someone's body language.

How can you thrive as a highly sensitive person?

How do you harness this superpower of yours? Turning it from a weakness to a strength? Here is my quick-fire list of ways:

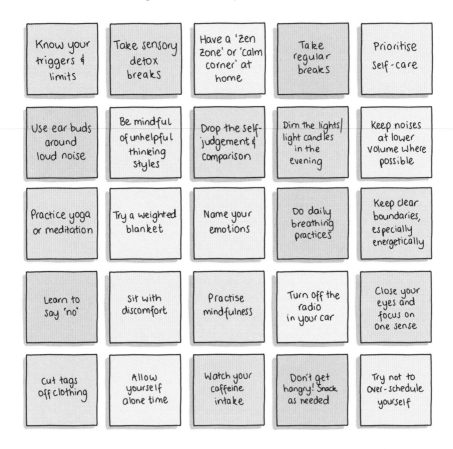

Know your triggers & limits	Take sensory detox breaks	Have a 'zen zone' or 'calm corner' at home	Take regular breaks	Prioritise self-care
Use ear buds around loud noise	Be mindful of unhelpful thinking styles	Drop the self-judgement & comparison	Dim the lights/ light candles in the evening	Keep noises at lower volume where possible
Practice yoga or meditation	Try a weighted blanket	Name your emotions	Do daily breathing practices	Keep clear boundaries, especially energetically
Learn to say 'no'	Sit with discomfort	Practise mindfulness	Turn off the radio in your car	Close your eyes and focus on one sense
Cut tags off clothing	Allow yourself alone time	Watch your caffeine intake	Don't get hangry! Snack as needed	Try not to over-schedule yourself

One thing you will need to practise as an empath is distinguishing between emotions that are yours and emotions that belong to others. As an empath, with your mirror neurons firing, you are prone to picking up on the emotions and energy of others. Practise asking yourself, 'Is this feeling mine?' If not, say: 'This feeling does not belong to me. I am not responsible for the emotions of others. I do not need to fix this feeling or figure it out. I allow it to flow over me.'

Create a decompression routine

When you come home from a long and stressful day, take ten or fifteen minutes to decompress, rather than diving straight into the tasks of cooking dinner, housework, sorting the kids and so on. A ritual where you disentangle yourself from the chaos and overwhelm of the day might be as simple as taking ten deep breaths, physically brushing yourself off and saying, 'I leave my day and work behind now. I step back into my peace and power.' And then make yourself a cup of herbal tea to enjoy on your own. Quietly. Mindfully. Maybe even in the shower with the door locked, like I do!

Be mindful of technology

As an HSP, it's good to be especially mindful of distractions like technology and mindless scrolling as an attempt to soothe yourself. While you may feel relaxed because you are getting some alone time or down-time, your brain actually finds this stimulating and what you are seeing as you scroll or watch TV may even be subtly activating your threat

do you begin to feel irritable?

do you feel foggy in the head?

does your chest tighten?

does your breathing change?

does a muscle group tighten up?

do you feel fatigued and unmotivated?

response. Learn to tune into your nervous system to notice signs it is becoming overloaded, and intervene with calming activities early.

Final reminders for highly sensitive people

- Know that it is okay if you prefer one-on-one interaction or more meaningful connections. You don't have to have a big group of friends or love crowds and parties.

- Become good at self-care and prioritising yourself. HSPs tend to engage in self-sacrifice and sometimes struggle to identify what they need to do to keep their emotional-wellbeing tank topped up.

- Self-care is CRUCIAL for HSPs; not a luxury!

- Recognise this is just a trait and one part of who you are — it is not a flaw or a diagnosis.

> HSPs tend to engage in self-sacrifice and sometimes struggle to identify what they need to do to keep their emotional-wellbeing tank topped up.

People-Pleasing

You've seen the term 'people-pleasing' mentioned a few times throughout this book. You've read about how your nervous system is involved, and how this trait may show up in your attempts to set boundaries or your tendencies to perfectionism. Let's explore people-pleasing a little more here; specifically looking at all the different ways this might show up in your life and how you can overcome it.

Remember that people-pleasing may develop for many different reasons, usually as a way of protecting yourself or trying to connect with others. Perhaps you had to learn to pick up on the emotions of those around you because of your parents. Maybe they were unpredictable, or neglectful or abusive. Or maybe a parent took up all the space because of their own addictions or mental-health struggles. In any of these circumstances, your ability to read and anticipate their emotions meant you could then edit your own behaviour in order to keep them happy and yourself safe. This could have been safety in a very real, physical sense or it could have been more about connection; when you altered yourself and kept them happy, they were more loving, giving of their time or seemed to accept you more.

Maybe in your childhood or teen years you were bullied or picked on. You learnt that in order to be liked or fit in you had to shrink yourself, or change the way you looked, dressed, acted and your interests in the world. Maybe you kept yourself safe by doing things for your peers and learnt that you had to abandon yourself and give to others without limit in order to be accepted.

It's possible people-pleasing started as a result of unhealthy or toxic relationships. You may have begun to alter who you were in order to be loved and connected with your partner, taking on their interests as your own, putting aside your own needs because you were never treated as a priority, doing everything for them because that's what your parents modelled or because the balance and equality was unequal and unfair. Over the years, these types of relationships chipped away at your sense of self and your confidence to be accepted and loved for who you are.

> Women often fall into people-pleasing roles because of wider societal and patriarchal narratives.

Under a wider lens, women often fall into people-pleasing roles because of wider societal and patriarchal narratives — we are called bossy or bitchy if we voice our opinions, we are called aggressive if we assert our boundaries and needs, we are called difficult if we speak up at work. We are accepted and told we are 'nice' and 'easygoing' when we go with the flow, meeting others' needs above our own and serving others. These behaviours are often reinforced and praised — even expected of — in females.

Looking at all of these things, you can see how easily you might adopt people-pleasing as a reflexive and habitual way of being. It often becomes the way that we seek and maintain connection with others and validation in our relationships. Others benefit greatly from those of us with a people-pleasing nature, and they're often unaware that underneath it all we are suffering and putting ourselves aside, abandoning or completely losing touch with our own wants, needs, values and desires.

You might know instantly in reading the heading of this section that you are a people-pleaser. If you're not sure, here are some of the ways people-pleasing might show up and present itself in your life. Check off which of these apply to you.

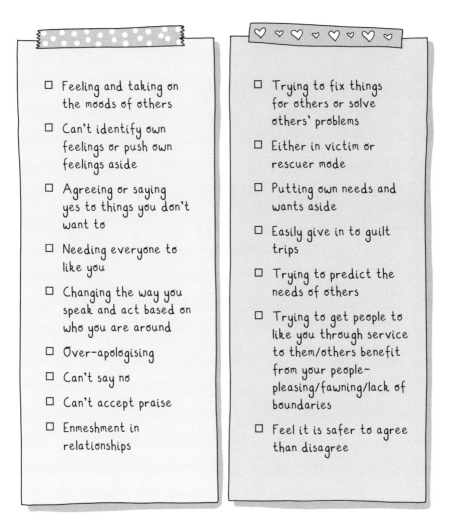

- ☐ Feeling and taking on the moods of others
- ☐ Can't identify own feelings or push own feelings aside
- ☐ Agreeing or saying yes to things you don't want to
- ☐ Needing everyone to like you
- ☐ Changing the way you speak and act based on who you are around
- ☐ Over-apologising
- ☐ Can't say no
- ☐ Can't accept praise
- ☐ Enmeshment in relationships

- ☐ Trying to fix things for others or solve others' problems
- ☐ Either in victim or rescuer mode
- ☐ Putting own needs and wants aside
- ☐ Easily give in to guilt trips
- ☐ Trying to predict the needs of others
- ☐ Trying to get people to like you through service to them/others benefit from your people-pleasing/fawning/lack of boundaries
- ☐ Feel it is safer to agree than disagree

Here are some common thoughts/beliefs of people-pleasers:

- 'I don't do conflict.'
- 'I'm easygoing.'
- 'I go with the flow.'
- 'I'm super low maintenance.'
- 'I'm too sensitive.'
- 'My needs don't matter.'
- 'I'm unlovable/unworthy.'
- 'I can't do boundaries.'/ 'I'm not good at boundaries.'
- 'They can't do XYZ without me.'
- 'I'm the peacekeeper in the family.'
- 'I have to fix people.'
- 'It's my fault if others feel XYZ.'
- 'I'd rather be put out/ uncomfortable than put someone else out.'

Here are some common somatic experiences of people-pleasers:

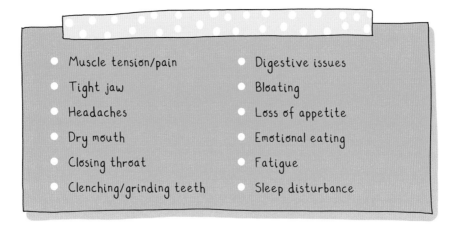

- Muscle tension/pain
- Tight jaw
- Headaches
- Dry mouth
- Closing throat
- Clenching/grinding teeth
- Digestive issues
- Bloating
- Loss of appetite
- Emotional eating
- Fatigue
- Sleep disturbance

Maybe you're seeing yourself reflected in these lists and realising that you are in a pattern of people-pleasing. Despite that, you might be thinking it is just easier to stay the course and carry on as you are — after all, does it really matter? What are the results of people-pleasing, anyway? Well . . . this.

- Burnout through taking on more than you need to/can handle.

- Ignoring your own needs and wants creates wider and long-lasting impacts on your sense of self-worth.

- Putting aside or not knowing your own values and priorities.

- Feeling unsure of who you really are because you're constantly changing yourself to please others and fit in.

- Your body lives in a constant threat response, including heightened somatic symptoms like digestive issues, muscle tension or pain that you don't realise is related.

- You experience unstable relationships/friendships as you are not being your true authentic self and you live in fear of disappointing others or losing relationships if you don't do what they want.

- You end up holding resentment towards others as your boundaries are stepped all over (and they are likely unaware they are even doing so).

- You feel a disconnection with own emotions after always pushing them down.

- Social burnout/fatiguing easily around others (it's exhausting when you're always reading others' emotions and trying to anticipate their needs).

- You experience fear and anxiety — especially the fear of judgement/rejection/abandonment.

So, how do you overcome these people-pleasing ways of yours? As with so many things, awareness is the key first step — acknowledge that you are doing it (quite possibly unconsciously up until now), and extend to yourself compassion and understanding as to why. This is a behaviour that you've 'practised' (maybe for years), and it has probably served past versions of yourself as a form of protection. It's okay for that to be true and for it to be time for you to let this go and step into your power. This acknowledgement will lead into you developing awareness of how people-pleasing shows up in your life now — where, with who, why?

Here are the next steps to overcoming people-pleasing:

- Soothe the nervous system first. As people-pleasing could be related to the fawn response (for more on that, see page 51), it is important to work on overall repair and safety in your body and nervous system. You might like to pay special attention to your body and somatic experience when you are in people-pleasing mode. Do you notice that your posture shifts, slumping inwards and collapsing through the spine and chest? You can begin nervous system regulation by shifting your posture, checking the tone of your voice, tuning in with your breathing and slowing this down, and practising general tools for activating the PNS (see pages 52–57 for more on this).

- There are usually limiting core beliefs that are tied up in your people-pleasing behaviours, so you'll need to do some work on digging those up and challenging them (you'll find all of this on pages 146–158).

- Keep your thinking styles in check (see pages 122–143 for more on this). Commonly you'll find mind reading, personalisation or shoulds involved in people-pleasing.

- Learn to set boundaries and say no. Start small and in insignificant relationships, and work your way into clear boundaries in all the relationships in your life (yes, there's a whole chapter on boundaries to help you, over on pages 178–194).

- Identify your own values and priorities. What really matters to you? What sparks joy? Do you honour these in your life and with your time? When we people-please, we often abandon our own likes and values and merge ourselves into others. Have you ever lied about loving a certain type of music or ended up spending time doing some activity you hate when you're in a new relationship? Of course we want to compromise and explore the interests of others, but not at the expense of losing who we are.

- PAUSE before you respond to a request or agree with/say yes to others — give yourself space to think about it. Say, 'I'll come back to you on that,' and then go away and think about whether you really do want to commit to this thing or you are reflexively saying yes in order to be liked. Ask yourself, 'Is this what I really want? If I say yes, what is my reason for saying yes? Do I really genuinely want to help, or do I feel obliged? Am I saying yes out of habit or as a people-pleasing response?'

- When asked to do something or someone says something and you're about to blindly nod along and agree, first notice and recognise how your body feels before you respond. If you notice signs of unease, this is your nervous system communicating with you!

- Learn to identify and sit with your own emotions.

- Identify your needs. Meet your own needs, or state these in relationships.

- Notice the draw to return to people-pleasing and old patterns that feel safe — the brain loves the familiar.

- Show up for yourself in the little things — this builds trust in self. People-pleasing and fawning can build years of disconnection from self, and a lack of self-trust or knowing of self.

- Connect actively or build new connections with safe people who validate and respect your needs/boundaries. Your ventral vagal system activates in safe social settings.

- Build a safe space for yourself — in your mind or physically in your home.

- Remember that you cannot control what others think or how they feel. Some of us slip into people-pleasing as a way to try to control others' reactions and perceptions of us, in order to feel safe.

Now I know that is a BIG list of things to think about, and that none of these changes will take place overnight. I encourage you to begin to get curious, observing yourself in relationships with others and slowly putting these healing strategies in place in your life. And, as with any change, sit with the guilt and discomfort that arises from all of this. It's natural, normal and expected that you will feel some tricky emotions and a pull to go back to your people-pleasing ways. You might like to lean on the affirmations on pages 252–253 as mantras to guide you in remembering your worth. Do it for YOU.

Summary

- Boundaries are key to building self-worth. They can be porous, rigid or flexible.

- Uphold your boundaries with others and yourself to build self-trust and worth.

- A yes is also a no. Remember: when you say yes to someone else, you are likely saying no to yourself.

- HSPs experience the world differently; this is a gift that can be nurtured.

- As an empath or HSP, it is important to protect your energy. Self-care is crucial.

- Regulating and soothing your nervous system is important for HSPs, empaths and people-pleasers — find ways to restore calm.

- People-pleasers will thrive if they work on boundaries — pausing before reacting, identifying their own needs, values and emotions, and practising sitting in the discomfort of not being able to control others through their actions.

CREATE HEALTHY HABITS

Creating healthy habits isn't always easy, and it's even harder to break the unhealthy and unhelpful ones! In this chapter you'll begin to understand why this is and build some solid foundations and skills to help you stick to your goals and create lasting changes.

Foundations

I distinctly remember working with a client in the very early years of my career in mental health. I was still studying at the time and was referred a young lady called Maddie who was struggling with high anxiety. With my limited experience, I was always nervous to work with new clients, hoping I would be able to help in some way or worrying I didn't know enough yet.

Case study

Maddie told me about her worries, the spiral of anxious thoughts she would get trapped in, and the avoidance behaviours that had begun in an effort to prevent a panic attack. I was sure that I could help her create some change, so we set about examining her unhelpful thinking styles, doing thought logs, challenging her beliefs, beginning some exposure work around avoidance . . . week after week she came back, reporting that she noticed some change but that ultimately, her body kept spiralling into an anxious and exhausted state.

I felt like I was failing her; why was nothing sticking? Why were we not getting any traction? It dawned on me that I had moved too fast — I had not looked at Maddie's life from a holistic perspective to understand her environment and all the other factors that form a multifaceted person. Suddenly, it started to make more sense . . .

Each morning Maddie woke up feeling utterly unrefreshed from her sleep after only managing to catch five or so hours. She would jump out of bed in a fury, running late, she would skip breakfast and drink three or four cups of coffee. On her way to study, she would pick up another coffee and race into her lessons.

Having woken late she had no time to pack lunch and being a poor student, funds were tight; she didn't eat until she got home. She would forget to drink water most days. Once home, she would have another coffee before eating packet noodles or a microwave pie as a bit of fuel to begin her homework assignments. After dinner, she would watch reruns of Friends (an attempt to leave behind the anxiety of the day) and eventually she would fall asleep, bleary-eyed and ruminating, at around 1 a.m.

Maddie had completely shaky, bordering on non-existent, foundations to support her mental health. She was running on caffeine (which was overstimulating her anxiety and nervous system), she drank no water, got no movement or exercise in her day and ate foods lacking in any nutritional value . . . it was no wonder that Maddie was feeling anxious and that nothing we were doing seemed to help much.

While your own daily routine might not be quite as lacking in foundations as Maddie's, you might be able to identify some of these things missing or lacking in your own life. You see, you can't start building a house from the attic! You start down at the foundations, making sure they are level, supportive and solid. Your foundations are: sleep, movement, nutrition and water.

What are your optimal foundations?

This will differ from person to person, and you'll have to experiment to find your own ideal level. But to give you an idea to work from:

Water eight cups a day (and cut back on that caffeine!)

Sleep seven to nine hours of quality uninterrupted sleep a night

Movement at least 30 minutes a day of some kind of movement or exercise

Nutrition a balanced diet, where you also make sure you are eating enough meals per day, e.g. three main meals plus snacks (listen to your hunger cues)

Imagine that this graph is actually a ball made up of four equal segments. If all four segments are the same, the ball is able to roll smoothly and hold its course. If all four segments are 'full' then the ball is able to roll easily. When the segments are deflated, the ball isn't as bouncy and resilient, and it rolls slowly.

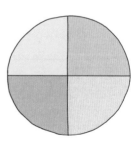

Here is someone who has pretty solid foundations

They drink enough water, get eight hours
of sleep a night, move their body most days
and eat a reasonably balanced diet. You can
see their ball is full and fairly even, meaning
this person has all the foundations in place to
allow things to run smoothly and support their
mental wellbeing.

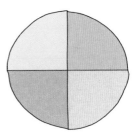

Here is someone with uneven foundations

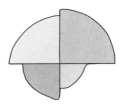

They don't drink enough during the day, get a
pretty good sleep each night but move their body
once a week at best and eat a poor diet, often
skipping meals or eating takeaways on the run.
You can see that their ball is uneven. If you were to roll it along, it
might tumble around in all directions and it certainly wouldn't get far.
This person's foundations make life roll along a little less smoothly
without a solid base in place to support their mental wellbeing.

It's easy to downplay the importance of making change like this.
You might think that 'just' getting some more sleep, or exercising
— or even trying other tools like breathing techniques, for example
— just aren't enough. It might feel like these things just 'won't touch
the sides' on the issues you are trying to overcome. But believe me:
I cannot stress enough how much change can take place when you
are scaffolding on top of a solid base.

For me, I need to know the science behind things in order to believe something will work. I have to know the why before I take action. So let me give you some fascinating information that might just motivate you to firm up those foundations of yours.

Why movement?

When you exercise and move your body, some wonderful things can happen for your mental health . . .

Why water?

Dehydration zaps your brain's energy and gets in the way of the production of serotonin (that feel-good hormone). Drinking water helps reduce the impact of stress and fatigue, decreases your risk of depression and anxiety, helps with mood swings and feelings of panic, and boosts your concentration.

Why sleep?

If you've ever been sleep-deprived, you will know first-hand the impact that lack of sleep has on your mental health: low mood, anxiety, irritability . . . the list goes on. It is absolutely crucial that you get enough sleep each night in order to support your wellbeing. Here's how your sleep cycles work while you're asleep:

So, if you are only getting five or six hours of sleep per night, or even less — or if you're waking up lots throughout the night and not completing a full sleep cycle or even getting into a deep sleep (thanks to things like wakeful children, high anxiety, insomnia or sleep apnoea) — then you're likely to feel the effects of this. You may struggle to regulate emotions or think clearly. When you're asleep, your brain processes information, memories and emotions. Just like you plug your phone in each night to recharge, sleep is your body's way of recharging your brain.

Why nutrition?

Each of these areas could really be a book of its own, and nutrition especially so. This book isn't the place to unpack nutrition fully (especially given I am not a nutritionist or doctor!), but what I will say is this:

- Nurturing your body by listening to your cues and feeding yourself when you are hungry is a great way to do some work on reparenting (the practice of giving your adult self what you missed out on as a child, by meeting your own emotional and physical needs) and looking after your inner child.

- Stress, depression and anxiety can cause an inflammatory response in your body. One way of helping to counteract that is by introducing more anti-inflammatory foods into your diet.

- Eating regular meals and snacks can help to keep your blood sugar level. Dips in blood sugar can leave us feeling shaky and anxious.

EXERCISE

Create your own foundation ball — if you were to rate the areas of sleep, movement, water and nutrition in your life in terms of how solidly you look after these areas, what would you rate them out of ten? Use the lines on the ball template here to colour in the number of segments to match each rating. Would your ball roll smoothly? Is it full and solid? Or is it deflated and uneven? This will give you a good baseline to work from and some feedback on the areas that might need a little love and attention.

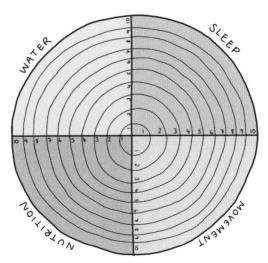

1 = I don't look after this need at all
10 = solid foundations in this area

A final note

There's another basic foundational need that I haven't included above (but deserves a mention due to its extreme importance): safety. It is a basic human need and right to feel safe. Now, this could be literal physical safety; knowing you are safe from violence, prejudice and harm of any kind. But it is also a feeling of safety in your own body and mind.

I believe so very many of us live in a constant state of dysregulation in terms of our nervous systems. We are jacked up and on edge, our lives are busy and we're always trying to do six things at one time, and as a result we live in a state of sympathetic nervous system activation (fight or flight). We aren't meant to live in that space for long periods of time. This state is supposed to be there to get us away from that sabre-toothed tiger! (For more on this, see page 48.) But these days, some of us are always 'on'.

What's more, if we are always 'on' we can actually end up with our parasympathetic nervous systems (specifically our vagus nerve) not functioning at their best. If you haven't read chapter 2 yet, you might be wondering 'What in the name of tacos is a vagus nerve,' you ask? Don't worry — I've got your back on page 46.

Habits

The neuroscience of habits and how we learn is something that I teach in each and every one of my coaching programmes. For me, it is so powerful because it explains:

- Why it is so hard to make and stick to new habits.

- Why we find ourselves falling back into old ways, even when we know they aren't good for us.

- Why we sometimes 'relapse' a long way down the track, when we made changes and have been doing things differently for a while.

Your brain contains billions of neurons. And these neurons talk to each other, firing off electrical impulses down their many interconnected pathways. Actions, thoughts and tasks we do often become strong and solid pathways, with neurons firing together over and over again — like a road map for our behaviours.

Let's simplify all this talk right down to this . . . imagine that this right here is a neuron. Let's call it Neuron A.

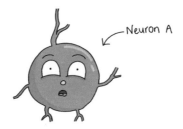

For the purpose of understanding behaviour and habits, let's say that Neuron A is what sparks off when your anxiety

is triggered. Maybe one day something comes up, you feel a pang of anxiety and you think, 'Oh my goodness, I can't cope.' And then you avoid the situation. When you do this, you create a new pathway in your brain — Neuron A talks to Neuron B.

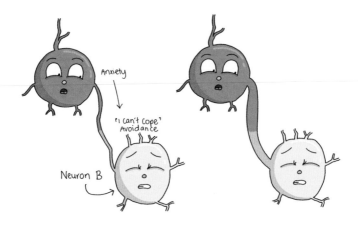

Maybe the next time your anxiety gets triggered, you remember that time you travelled down the pathway from A to B. It seemed like a valid way of coping, so you do it again. After a while of repeating this pattern — feel anxiety, then think 'I can't cope,' and then avoid something — you form a solid connection in your brain. The pathway has been travelled a whole bunch of times and it becomes very automatic. Very habitual. This pathway in your brain is like one of those four-lane super-highways where you can get in your car and go 100 kilometres an hour down it. You don't really have to think all that much; it's smooth, easy and you do it on autopilot.

Now, let's introduce Neuron C.

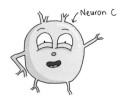

Maybe as you read this book you pick up a new tool, a new way of thinking, a new behaviour to try. Maybe your anxiety gets triggered one day and you think to yourself, 'Hang on, let me try that tool from Be Your Best Self. *I'm going to step into the discomfort, face the fear, breathe deep, challenge this thought . . .' (Whatever the thought is.) You go ahead and do it and WHAM — your brain makes a new connection: A to C. Making this new pathway feels a little bit like whacking your way through dense bush with a stick to make a new road — it's clunky and uncomfortable at first.*

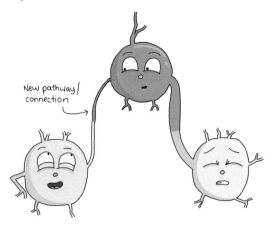

New pathway / connection

The next time your anxiety gets triggered, which of these two pathways are you more likely to take (A to B or A to C)? A to B, right?! So much easier, so much smoother! BUT let's say you push through and you try your new tool/behaviour/way of thinking again. When you travel that A to C path, it gets a little stronger. You do this again and again, opting to take your new healthy path. Over time, the path of whacked-through bush becomes a gravel track, and then a footpath, and then a shingled road, and then a concrete street and soon enough, it too becomes a highway. It now feels habitual and automatic.

Throughout the process you probably reverted back down the original A to B highway a number of times; maybe you were tired or emotional, and you forgot your new tool. Maybe your inner critic took over for a minute there? Whatever the reason; it makes sense. This highway still exists. Even though it might not be healthy or helpful, it is automatic and easy for you. This explains why we 'relapse'. It explains why it's so hard to break old habits and create new ones.

But do you know what? The more you use the new track, the easier it becomes. And the less you travel the old highway, the more that road begins to break down (basically, your brain doesn't like to waste space and energy on pathways that aren't being used). Over time, the pathways look like this:

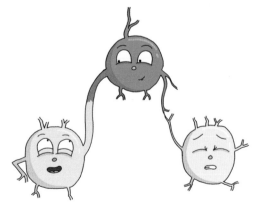

So remember:

- Hang in there when creating new habits and trying new ways of thinking and behaving. This is going to take time and repetition. It's worth it.

- You will 'slip up' sometimes; have compassion for this. It makes sense. It isn't worth beating yourself up over.

- Treat 'slip ups' and times you repeat your old behaviours as fascinating opportunities to learn: What went 'wrong'? What got in the way of me trying the new behaviour? Which thoughts stopped me? Which barriers are still here? What could I do differently next time?

- Learning new things feels clunky and uncomfortable at first. Do you remember when you learnt to ride a bike? What was at first a wobbly, terrifying disaster becomes something effortless. Even if you haven't ridden a bike in years and you got back on one now, you would instinctively know what to do thanks to that old highway you built!

How do you create habits that stick?

I want to give you a few simple ideas to support you in creating new habits. While it's useful to understand how new habits are created in the brain, it's sticking to these new habits that often trips us up. How can we remind ourselves to take this new pathway time and time again out there in the real world? How can we stop ourselves from travelling down that old pathway on autopilot?

Here's a look at some habit-creating tools I teach to my coaching clients — they are simple, and you can also have a lot of fun with them!

Habit Creator 1: Use Post-it notes

Post-it notes are your new friends! When you are trying to create a new habit, like taking mindful breaths throughout your day, checking in with your thoughts/emotions, drinking more water — whatever it is — pop Post-it notes around your space where you will see them to trigger the habit memory and cue you to take action. Stick your Post-it note reminders on your mirror, on the bathroom door, on the milk in the fridge, on the kettle, on the dash of your car . . . anywhere you know you will see it. After a few days, move the Post-it notes to new positions — otherwise your brain gets used to seeing them in a certain place and begins to gloss over and ignore them!

In my last coaching group, one of our members, Tash, wanted to introduce a more peaceful morning routine. Every morning when Tash woke up, she would go straight on her phone, checking work emails and spiralling into anxiety. Tash put a big purple Post-it note on the screen of her phone each night that said, 'Good morning! No phone use for 30 minutes.' She replaced the time spent scrolling in the morning with some deep breaths and a few sun salutations. Tash noticed a huge change in how her mornings unfolded and in her anxiety levels with this simple trick.

Habit Creator 2: Link it

Link your new habit with an existing one. Existing habits are already super-highways in your brain's neural circuitry — so if you can tack a new habit on to these, you effectively get to hitchhike your way to the new habit sticking! Here are some examples:

- You already have a habit of shuffling your way to the kettle each morning for a cuppa, right? So now, instead of checking your emails while you wait for the jug to boil, link a new habit (with your Post-it note reminder) of standing and watching the kettle boil while intentionally taking long, slow belly breaths.

- Your body habitually goes to the loo each day, without you thinking much about it. Pop a Post-it note opposite the toilet to remind you to mentally check in with your thoughts and emotions each time you take a seat on the proverbial throne!

- You habitually stand in front of your mirror each morning to brush your teeth or do your makeup. Link a new habit of saying mantras that ooze body acceptance, set daily intentions or repeat your daily gratitudes while you do this.

- Each evening, you take a shower or wash off your makeup before bed. Link the new habit of doing this mindfully, tuning into each action as you complete it and breathing slowly.

- Maybe you have an evening habit of taking the dog out for a stroll and a toilet break. Link a new habit of listening to a self-development podcast or some soothing music along the way.

These are just a few examples. You can link any habit you like!

Habit Creator 3: Alarm yourself!

I use the alarm on my phone or the task-reminder app for everything.

When you know that you have
someone else other than just yourself
to answer to, it is harder to sabotage
or ignore the new behaviour.

Honestly, if I didn't set myself reminders I would never take my supplements and I sure as heck wouldn't turn up to any of the meetings I set! You can use your alarms and reminders for new habits, too.

Schedule actions into your phone with a nice little alarm tone. Importantly, set these for times you are most likely to take action (don't set an alarm right when you know you will be busy and press snooze on it). We want to take action on the alarm and follow through — if you press dismiss when your alarm goes off each time, it becomes a meaningless intervention that won't create any new pathways (other than maybe one that reinforces dismissing and ignoring your reminders!).

Habit Creator 4: Be accountable

Get an accountability buddy! If you want to start a habit of going for a walk every second day, ask a friend or your partner to either come along with you or hold you accountable for following through with it. When you know that you have someone else other than just yourself to answer to, it is harder to sabotage or ignore the new behaviour.

How do you break old habits?
Habit Breaker 1: Break the circuit (my favourite and most fun habit breaker)

Break the neural pathway from playing out on autopilot by making yourself do something random or silly in the middle of your usual steps. Your brain is so used to following the steps of a habit from A to B without much thought. This is how humans work, going on to autopilot for tasks we have undertaken a million times. This makes sense — why use the brain power of thinking something through when you can just encode it to long-term memory and do it without thinking?! Our brains go on autopilot when we drive a car, ride a bike, make a cup of tea, get our toast ready in the morning and so on (any task you have done a hundred times, really). Your brain also goes on to autopilot with bad habits, like picking the ends of your hair when you are nervous, smoking, eating a block of chocolate when you watch TV, pressing 'next episode' on Netflix eight times in a row, scrolling mindlessly on social media, picking out your flaws each time you look in the mirror or jumping straight to self-criticism when you make a mistake. These are all habits, too.

How a circuit breaker works is by putting something fun, silly, or random (that requires you to actively think) in the middle of your autopilot routine. Let's say this is your bad behaviour routine, from A to B: you feel sad so you scroll mindlessly on your phone, ignoring your emotions, then eat a packet of biscuits and feel sick. Your circuit breaker looks like this: A to Z to maybe B, maybe not! Let's say Z, in this case, is putting on a beanie and gloves (totally random and ridiculous). So, you feel sad . . . You're just about to pick up your phone and you remember the circuit breaker; you aren't allowed to go to step B unless you go and put on a beanie and gloves first. You go and put them on, and now all of a sudden you are really thinking about the choice you get to make: 'Do I want to scroll? Do I really want to eat the whole packet?' This silly and simple action has thrown a spanner in the works and rerouted your autopilot.

How a circuit breaker works is by putting something fun, silly, or random (that requires you to actively think) in the middle of your autopilot routine.

You can, of course, choose the old habit — and if you do, you are doing this very intentionally, fully aware of your actions and the consequence. What is more likely is that you'll have a laugh at your furry glove-covered hands and decide to do something more productive.

Here are some more fun examples from sessions with my coaching clients:

- Wear a hat or tiara. One client, Natalie, decided to break her old habit of picking at her hair nervously and scratching at her skin. When she felt the urge, she would first go and put on a glorious top hat or tiara. She felt so funny in her headdress that she never followed through with her unhelpful impulse and would instead go and meditate or take a walk.

- Put on lipstick. My client Priya found that she would get into terrible negative thinking spirals when she was cleaning and tending to the house; her brain didn't need to focus on the task and so would wander off into worries or harsh thoughts about herself. She decided to put on bright red lipstick and a dress while she cleaned, which broke the old pathway and made her mindful of her thoughts as she went about unloading the dishwasher.

- Make the bed behind you. Another client, Dee, had a habit of pressing snooze on her alarm each morning. She would hit snooze up to eight times before finally getting up, and was always running late to work. Her circuit breaker consisted of her putting her phone on the other side of the room, and when she got up to snooze it she would quickly make the bed behind her and put on pants she had laid out the night before. This shocked her brain, which still desperately wanted to go back to bed, but it was too late — the pants were on and the covers were neatly tucked in! So, she ended up staying up and having an extra 30 minutes to get ready each morning.

Habit Breaker 2: Narrate it

State out loud the behaviour or habit you are about to engage in. Naming and narrating your actions, thoughts and the behaviour can be enough to bring your attention and awareness to it and change your mind about following through. For example you might say, 'I'm about to get up and get a whole tub of ice-cream out of the freezer and stalk my ex on Facebook.' Now . . . if that doesn't give you a moment of reflection, I don't know what will!

I hope these habit makers and circuit breakers give you a few ideas of how you might begin to dismantle those old patterns of yours and begin to compassionately build new ones.

Above all else, what I hope you take from this chapter is some self-compassion and understanding. All of us struggle to break old habits. All of us have to work hard to create new ones. Sometimes people make it look like change or their success came easy, like it just fell into their lap, and this makes us feel like we are getting it wrong. We ask ourselves, 'Why do I find it so hard to do XYZ when it comes so easy to them? What's wrong with me?!' And on top of this, we layer on the guilt as we engage in the blame−shame game with ourselves. Let me tell you that most of those 'instant successes' and 'easy wins' are all show. You do have to work at what you want. And the best way to do that is to be kind to yourself, show up for yourself, and give yourself love and compassion along the way.

> Sometimes people make it look like change or their success came easy, like it just fell into their lap, and this makes us feel like we are getting it wrong.

Summary

- Don't ignore your foundations. They are the key building block to solid mental wellbeing. Focus on making sure you are drinking enough water, getting enough sleep and moving and nourishing your body.

- Building a new habit takes repetition. It's normal for it to feel clunky and a bit hard or uncomfortable at first.

- The more you repeat something, the more developed, automatic and ingrained the behaviour becomes.

- It's normal to fall back into old habits and patterns thanks to well-formed neural pathways. Have compassion for yourself when this happens, and learn from these times.

LEARN
TO LOVE
YOURSELF

Learning to love yourself means learning to care for yourself, speaking to yourself with words of love and kindness, nurturing your inner child and getting to know the shadow parts of yourself that came to exist in order to protect you. In this chapter you'll be exploring self-care, affirmations, your inner child and your protection parts. What a beautiful way to round out your journey in this book — with love and compassion!

Self-Love & Self-Care

Imagine that this watering can is your emotional capacity — your watering can of resilience, if you will.

When your watering can is full, you are operating at full capacity. You feel on top of things, you bounce back easily and you are able to support others because you have the bandwidth to carry more of an emotional load. There are lots of things in life that require you to pour from your watering can (giving your energy, your time, or even depleting you).

Supporting your partner

Raising your children

Being there for your family

work

Connecting with your friends

An argument with a loved one

keeping on top of your to-do list

Dealing with 'life dramas'

. . . the list goes on. All of these things require 'watering' in order for them to flourish (or in order for you to resolve them and get through them), and we can do that — our watering cans were designed for it.

Now, we can't keep making all these withdrawals from our watering can without re-filling it, right? Let's introduce 'the well of resilience' or your 'self-care well', if you will.

This well represents the things that 'top us back up' and 'fill our buckets' — things like exercise, nutrition, self-care, hobbies that nourish us, meditation, mindfulness, healthy boundaries, date nights, therapy, a good yarn with a supportive friend, living in line with our values and needs, getting a good night's sleep, and so on. This exchange works  well when everything is going smoothly. We water the things in our life that need attention and care, then we fill ourselves back up — and the cycle goes around and around in our happy little gardens.

But . . . sometimes the demand for water goes up. Suddenly we are faced with things that require us to pour more and more from our watering cans. Maybe someone in your family gets sick and needs care, maybe a friend is going through a hard time and leans heavily on you, maybe you are in a financial pickle, maybe you are short-staffed at work, maybe your relationship is going through a rough patch or maybe you go through a period of struggling with your own mental health. Any number of things can drain your watering can. And sometimes more than one of these things happens at the same time.

Now, if you are able to meet the demand by getting back to your well to top up your watering can, you might be all right. In these times of high stress and demand, you need to increase your self-care and pay special attention to the things that keep you 'topped up'. However, what often happens when we find ourselves under strain is that we forget to meet the increased demand. We are so frantic running around watering all of these other areas in our life that we forget to top up our watering can!

You wind up with an empty watering can, neglecting yourself — and the other things in your life begin to suffer, too.

Time for some home truths (you know I say it all with love!). Some of us keep pouring from an empty watering can unconsciously. Others do this by choice. This choice can relate to our limiting beliefs; things like 'my needs don't matter', 'I have to put others' needs above mine', 'if I put myself first it's selfish', 'if I don't serve others they'll reject me', 'my worth is tied up in pleasing other people', 'my value is determined by what others think of me' and so on.

If pouring from an empty watering can for you comes from a place of people-pleasing, consider this: how well do you serve relationships when you are showing up in those relationships empty and depleted? How well do you serve others when you show up for those people not full and overflowing yourself? If your motivation for not engaging in self-care and topping yourself up is the excuse 'I have to keep everyone else happy', then it might be time to take a step back and realise you aren't actually bringing your best self to the table. How would they feel if they knew you felt depleted but

We human beings are made to
live in connection with others,
and these relationships naturally
require work and effort from us.

kept serving them? Probably guilty, maybe upset . . . that's not really serving others either, is it? Make it a priority to top yourself up to a point of feeling content and resilient. Then I'm sure you could bring a much better version of yourself to the people in your life.

Maybe you don't top up your watering can because you are holding on to some notion of stoicism: 'I don't need help. I can do it all by myself.' If this is you, ask yourself where this idea came from. And then drop it. Remind yourself that humans are designed to live in connection with others.

The solution to a depleted watering can is to increase your self-care as the demand and stress in your life goes up. You can't change the fact that there will be things in life that require you to pour from your watering can. We human beings are made to live in connection with others, and these relationships naturally require work and effort from us. We wouldn't want this to change. Healthy connections and meaningful work are a huge part of what keeps us mentally well. However, in life things naturally ebb and flow, and there will be times when the balance goes out the window and the demand for your capacity goes up greatly. It is in these times that we need to make sure our watering cans are topped up.

Make it a daily practice to check in on your watering can: 'How much have I poured out today versus how much have I topped up?' Keep a mental tally and be mindful of striving for a balance here.

Having intentional daily practices is a good way to establish a habit and routine of topping up your watering can.

When the watering can is empty, it takes a real effort to get it back up to capacity again. An empty watering can is burnout. And trying to get back on track from this place is like an 'ambulance at the bottom of the cliff' approach. What we want is a 'fence at the top of the cliff' approach: putting in smaller amounts of effort here and there, taking small moments out of your day to nourish your mental wellbeing. This is a proactive and preventative approach.

How do you keep your watering can topped up?

How you keep your watering can topped up is up to you! There are lots of ideas and things to reflect on in this book to help you do that. So, for this chapter, I would like to introduce you to just a few simple tools to top up your watering can with small daily practices. Have a read-through and pick just one or two that you might like to try (you certainly don't need to do them all!).

Daily practice 1: Mindful mornings

The morning is often a time of increased anxiety for people — cortisol is at its highest between 6 a.m. and 8 a.m. We wake up with our minds full of to-do lists and the worries of the day ahead. Before we even get out of bed, we've used our cellphones to check our emails, peruse the daily news and scroll on social media — all things that switch on the threat response and set us up for a day of depletion. Here are some ways to make your mornings mindful:

- Say no to the scroll! Don't go on your cellphone for at least 30 minutes after waking.

- Move intentionally slowly, completing one task at a time instead of trying to eat breakfast while simultaneously doing your makeup and answering emails; get up earlier if you need to.

- Switch from regular coffee to decaf, especially if you are someone who feels anxious or keyed-up and on-edge.

- Make sure you eat breakfast — keep those blood sugars level! Low/dropping blood sugar can be part of the reason you feel anxious.

- Create some calming rituals or routines and weave those into your morning, like diffusing an essential oil, taking a shower, laying your clothes out the night before, having a to-do list ready, meditation or a breathing practice. These don't have to take up a lot of time — do your breathing technique while you make a cup of tea, meditate for two minutes before you get out of bed, repeat some mantras or gratitudes in the shower, etc.

Daily practice 2: Gratitude

Combat your negativity bias with gratitude. Thanks to our old prehistoric brains with their caveman software, humans naturally keep an eye out for things that are going wrong or might be a threat (a great function when your survival depended on it!). This means it is much easier for us to focus on the negative things in life. Of course, the media knows this too and majorly overcapitalises on it, constantly bombarding us with terrifying and miserable news . . . and images of people living 'better lives' in smaller-sized jeans than us, all for the purpose of keeping us glued to our screens or buying more. Our brains absolutely lap all of this up. Have you ever found

> Thanks to our old prehistoric brains with their caveman software, humans naturally keep an eye out for things that are going wrong or might be a threat.

yourself watching something shocking on TV, and while you don't want to see it you somehow find yourself unable to turn away? That survival brain of yours just can't help itself. It thinks it needs to take in all of this negativity in order to keep you safe. But ultimately, with the society we live in today, where we can be bombarded by threats and bad news everywhere we turn, this tendency only leads us into feeling stressed and depressed.

So, part of the solution is acknowledging and becoming aware of the brain's tendency to search for the negative and then counteracting it. That's where gratitude comes in. Below are some ways you could incorporate gratitude as a daily practice.

- Gratitude journal: Fill out three things or more that you are grateful for each day in a journal.

- Grateful grub: Before each meal, say a quiet word of thanks — for the food, and to your body for absorbing the nutrients and keeping you going.

- Family gratitude: During some family time, like when you sit down to dinner, each person in your household takes a turn to mention something they are grateful for.

- Shower of gratitude: Anytime you take a shower, either scan through each part of your body and list something you are grateful to it for, or take a moment to think about what you were grateful for that day.

- Post-it notes of thanks: Each and every day, write on a Post-it note something you are grateful for from your day. Put these Post-it notes up on a wall or in a jar, and review them when you need a pick-me-up — perhaps monthly or yearly.

- Glimmering gratitudes: At times when you feel particularly overcome with thanks, jot this down on a Post-it note for the wall or in a journal so you can review your most glimmering moments when you need to remember the good things in life.

- Daily review: In a journal, or with your household at dinner time, review these two points: What didn't go to plan today and what did I learn? What went well today?

Daily practice 3: Mindful moments

There are a million ways to weave and integrate mini mindful moments, or micro-mindfulness practices into your day.

- You could try a mindful bite. Savour the first moment of any meal by tuning in to observe textures and smells, and really relish in the tastes of that first mouthful.

- Try a mindful cup of tea. As you drink your tea, notice the smell, the way it looks, the way the cup feels in your hands, the taste in your mouth and so on.

- Do your chores mindfully. As you are going about your routines of the day, do your chores mindfully — even if this is as simple as unloading the dishwasher, you can notice the way that feels, the way it sounds, what your hands are touching and so on.

Daily practice 4: Foundations

Drink water. Nourish your body. Get enough sleep. Move.

Daily practice 5: Mindful screen time

Get intentional about how you use your devices. Quite often we mindlessly scroll or tune out while binging a TV series as a way of detaching from reality and emotions. Now, don't get me wrong, I love a good Netflix binge session as much as the next person! But this screen time can easily slide into the 'unhealthy range' when we use it as our only coping strategy, or as a way of not facing up to our emotions and worries.

Start by putting boundaries around your screen/device use in the mornings and evenings. A great rule to try is no screens 30 minutes before bed or right after waking.

Here are some other hints to keep your scrolling in check:

- Use a screen-time notification app or check your stats in your phone's settings.

- Put mindless binge apps (like social media) into a separate folder and not on your home screen. Even just having to scroll across and go into a folder to find the app can be enough to break the autopilot your thumb seems to go on!

- Delete certain apps for periods of the week; delete Instagram from Sunday to Wednesday, for example.

- Take a detox. Delete certain apps for a period of time, or leave the phone behind for a day.

- Set yourself phone-check times. Decide on certain periods of the day when you will allow yourself to check for notifications or social media. For instance, check notifications at 9 a.m., 1 p.m., 4 p.m. and 7 p.m., or social media time is between 7 p.m. and 7.30 p.m. daily.

Daily practice 6: Self-checks

How often do you find yourself on autopilot in your day? Sometimes the demands of our ever-increasing to-do lists and busy schedules have us running from A to Z all day long without ever stopping to take a breath and check in with ourselves. A simple daily practice to help you become more in tune with your needs, and to help you integrate your mind-body experience, is a 'self-check'. Set an alarm on your cellphone to go off at three different times in the day. Make sure you try to pick a time when you know you are more likely to respond to the alarm; don't set the alarm when you know you'll be cooking dinner or in meetings and will probably just press snooze and ignore it. This alarm is your prompt to pause and ask yourself a series of simple questions:

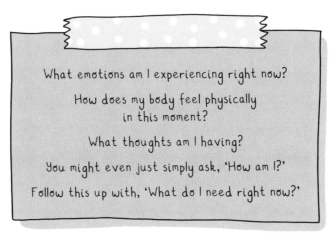

What emotions am I experiencing right now?

How does my body feel physically in this moment?

What thoughts am I having?

You might even just simply ask, 'How am I?'

Follow this up with, 'What do I need right now?'

This practice puts a stop to us steamrollering through our days without a thought about our internal experience or our needs. Sometimes you'll find that all is well, and what you 'need right now' is just to carry on. Other times you'll find that your body is feeling hungry, you've forgotten to eat and you need to take a break. Other times you'll stumble across a big feeling, like stress, and what you need is to take a few deep breaths.

Daily practice 7: Connect

We are wired for connection. We are not designed to exist as islands without support and community around us. Our nervous systems thrive when we feel safe, supported and connected in relationships. When our nervous systems are under threat and we feel unsafe, we find this connection difficult and we withdraw. So make a point to connect with someone each day. That might be sending a few messages back and forth with an old friend, organising a date night with your partner, having a ten-minute period of connection and play with your child without distractions, or having a long hug with a loved one or a friendly conversation with a coworker over lunch.

Which other daily practices do you think would work for you? Take some time to reflect on what a typical day looks like for you now, and how you could enhance that. Make your daily practices intentional, nourishing, centred around you and your needs, and achievable. And, if you don't manage them on any given day, take this as a learning opportunity — NOT an opportunity to let your inner critic run rampant or your perfectionism step in to sabotage your efforts!

Affirmations

I want to dedicate this section to lavishing you with some affirmations to inspire, comfort and uplift you. Before I do, here are some ideas for how you could weave affirmations into your life:

- Write out your favourites on Post-it notes and pop them around your house.

- Write them on your mirror.

- Type them into your phone as reminders that pop up randomly in your week.

- Take a picture from this book and set it as your lock-screen background on your phone or your laptop.

- Repeat some out loud to yourself to start your day.

- Rehearse some in your mind when you're looking in the mirror and brushing your teeth before bed.

- Repeat comforting affirmations in times of anxiety or stress to calm and centre your thoughts.

One last thing before we get to the affirmations: sometimes clients will say they struggle with affirmations, so I want to help trouble-shoot a few of the challenges that pop up often.

> **Q:** *I struggle with affirmations because I just don't believe them. What do I do when it just doesn't feel true?*
> **A:** *When an affirmation is too far removed from your current reality or beliefs, it creates cognitive dissonance (you might remember this term from pages 28–29 about our inner*

critics). If this is happening for you, you might have some more growth and work to do towards believing it, and that's okay. In the meantime, as you work towards that, change the affirmation to feel more realistic for you. For example, if the mantra 'I am deeply and innately worthy' just doesn't sit right with you, you could change it to 'I am working on realising that my worth is not tied to external factors', 'all people are worthy' or 'I am building my self-worth every day'.

Q: *When I repeat affirmations in the mirror, I feel very emotional. What's up with that?*
A: *Hearing words of love towards yourself might be completely new to you. This can bring up discomfort along with any number of other emotions. Ask yourself: 'Can I lean into this discomfort? Can I push through, sitting with these words and these emotions?' The tears may be speaking to wounded parts of yourself that are releasing tension and emotion after finally being acknowledged or spoken to with kindness. Go easy on yourself here too; start small. If it's all too much, it's okay to step back and look after yourself, without flooding yourself and becoming overwhelmed.*

Q: *My affirmations aren't working! Why don't I feel better?*
A: *A few things could be happening here:*
1) You don't believe the affirmations or you're just going through the motions. Pick affirmations that you feel you can connect to and want to believe. Change them if they just don't seem to be hitting the mark.
2) You aren't saying them often enough; if you only try them out

once or twice, nothing much will happen. Your brain needs to hear things over and over.

3) Your affirmations are outnumbered. If you take one minute out in the morning for affirmations, then spend the rest of the day listening to your inner critic and thinking negatively, the affirmations just won't work.

Pick affirmations that you feel you can connect to and want to believe.

When using affirmations, you can also use your imagination to create a picture of you succeeding in your mind. For example, if you have a public-speaking gig coming up and are worried about it, repeat the affirmation 'I am confident and capable when I speak' and picture yourself at this presentation, walking confidently on to the stage, smiling, looking open and brave, speaking well, engaging your audience and finishing to claps and smiles. You see, your brain doesn't really understand the difference between reality and what we are imagining, and will react in the same way to your fantasies as it would to real life. This is why, when you are only thinking about your worries or fears, your body reacts with a rush of butterflies, feeling sick and nervous. Your amygdala reacts as though these fears are really happening. You can use this superpower of the mind to your advantage — imagine things going well, imagine yourself as confident, imagine yourself succeeding. Creating these images can have a powerful effect, not only on your mood but also on the outcome of your worries.

Let's get into the affirmations! You could pick a handful of these that resonate most with you to put into use in your life. Now — this is important. If any of these just don't sit right with you, creating that cognitive dissonance, leaving you feeling like you aren't doing it right or they just plain don't help because you don't believe them . . . try putting something like 'I am working on believing that . . .' in front of them.

Affirmations

I am capable.

I am strong.

I am confident.

I already have everything I need within me to succeed.

My worth is not determined by external factors.

I am deeply and innately worthy.

I deserve to feel love and belonging.

I am conquering my fears.

I am calm and at peace.

I am worthy of respect.

My voice matters.

My needs matter.

I hold firm to my boundaries.

I can get through hard times.

Wellbeing is a practice I am committed to.

I listen to my body and give it what it needs.

I allow my emotions space.

I can ask for help when I need it.

I value myself.

I deserve to feel happiness.

I deserve rest — it does not need to be earned.

I am grateful to my body for all the functions it performs for me.

Progress over perfection.

My worth is not defined by my achievements.

I am a work in progress. I don't expect perfection.

My confidence does not depend on what others think of me.

Setbacks and challenges are opportunities for learning and growth.

I can notice and sit with my feelings.

My boundaries matter. I can say no.

I deserve to say yes to myself.

I can stick to my goals and create new habits.

I am not responsible for other people's emotions.

I can let go of the things that are not within my control.

Feelings are not facts.

Not all thoughts are true.

I am the observer of my thoughts.

Your Inner Child

There is a fascinating model of therapy called Transactional Analysis (TA), developed by Eric Berne during the 1950s. TA examines social interactions and relationships and analyses the 'transactions' that take place within those. One theory within TA that I find interesting is the concept that internally we have three ego states: a parent ego state, a child ego state and an adult ego state. Each of these ego states has its own behaviours and ways of thinking and feeling. I'll use the diagram opposite to explain further.

This model seeks to explain how when we are interacting with others, ideally we do so when we are both operating from our adult ego state. However, sometimes we may speak to someone from our critical parent state, possibly eliciting in them a response from their adapted child state, and so on. While this theory was designed around the interactions between two people, the idea that intrigues me most is that we actually relate to and within ourselves from these different ego states.

Each of us has this child-like ego state within us. And I can vouch for this myself here; while I would love to tell you I always come from a place of rational level-headed logic and am always in control of my emotional responses . . . I just can't! There are absolutely times (often!) when I come from my parent or child ego state in the way I relate to myself. Here's a scenario to illustrate this:

I launch a new course in my business and the sales don't go as well as I had hoped. Internally I say to myself, 'You see? You don't know what you're doing in your business and you're going to fail. You might as well remove the course; it was a

EGO STATES

PARENT

Behaviours, thoughts & feelings that come from this ego state may be copied from our own parental figures. Within this state we have 2 ways of operating:

NURTURING PARENT

Loving & responds with kindness & caring

CRITICAL PARENT

Scolds, judges or controls

ADULT

Behaviours, thoughts & feelings that come from this ego state are direct responses to the here & now & tend to be rational.

CHILD

Behaviours, thoughts & feelings that come from this ego state may be replayed from our own childhoods. Like the Parent ego state, within this state we have 2 ways of operating:

FREE CHILD

Creative, playful & adventurous

ADAPTED CHILD

conforms to others' needs or rebels

waste of time!' Which ego state do you see here? The critical parent, right? (Which is very similar to our inner critic — in fact, I'm sure they are one and the same.)

I might also respond like this: 'Well, I suck!' Then impulsively delete the course, and go off and sulk for the day. Which ego state would this be? The adapted child, right? Skulking away in a corner and throwing a tantrum!

The ideal place for me to come from is a place of logical compassion — my adult ego state — sounding something like this: 'This hasn't gone as I planned, and that's okay. This is a good learning opportunity. I can debrief on what went well and what didn't.'

I might also come from a nurturing parent ego state. I might not be as rational or effective from this place, but I would be so much more compassionate: 'Oh, that's so disappointing. Poor me, I deserve a cup of tea and to take the rest of the day off.'

What I want to focus on in this chapter, with TA in mind, is our child ego states. The 'little you' that lives inside of you, as an adult, that needs love and nurturing.

Sometimes these child states have been wounded in some way; they might feel vulnerable, or maybe they didn't have their needs met growing up. Here's the thing: we could easily become stuck in a 'victim mindset' when we think about our child ego states, thinking, 'I've been hurt. It's everyone else's fault that I'm damaged.' (Please note, this does not apply to those who were abused and victimised as children, or at any point in their lives. This was not your fault and this was done to you.)

You are in charge. You are responsible for your own healing, meeting your own needs and setting boundaries for yourself.

When I think about my own inner child, this doesn't just apply to me between the ages of birth and ten, for example. I think of myself operating from this child-like ego state in my teens and even into my early twenties. All of these times in your life can use your re-parenting and inner child work. But what I want us to all feel clear on is this: you are now an adult. You are in charge. You are responsible for your own healing, meeting your own needs and setting boundaries. In doing this work, you are helping to nurture and heal your inner child. Let's explore some ways we can do this.

How do you re-parent yourself?

While we may all desperately deserve and wish we had the 'perfect parents', in actual fact you were raised by humans. Humans with flaws, who were likely doing the best they could at the time with what they knew and the resources they had. They probably didn't meet every one of your needs all the time. No one can. They probably messed up here and there. Everyone does. They probably didn't prioritise you all the time. That's hard to do. They probably said the wrong things. They were operating from their own past scripts and maybe even re-enacting the parenting they received. None of this serves to invalidate any pain or suffering you endured. That happened. That was real and your responses and emotions around this are allowed and valid.

What I want to offer you is the idea that you, as an adult, now get to be your very own loving parent. But how?

Speak to your inner child

Close your eyes right now and imagine a younger you — maybe this is you as a child, maybe you're in your late teens. Picture a version of yourself that is going through a tough time and needs love and care. Breathe deeply into your belly and place one hand over your heart. Picture yourself now, compassionate and loving, wrapping this younger-you in a warm embrace. Imagine asking younger-you, 'What do you need?' Now sit quietly and allow space to see what comes up in response to this question.

Treat yourself now how you would treat a small child, or how you wish you were treated as a child

I created a post on this some time back for my Instagram community, and to this day it remains one of the most popular. Here are some ideas of how to translate this into practice:

- Take care of yourself and your needs.

- If you are hungry, nourish your body.

- If you are thirsty, listen. Get yourself some water.

- If you are upset or in tears, give yourself hugs, space, love and compassion.

- If you are tired, listen to your body. Go to bed early. Take a nap. Tuck yourself in between your sheets and shut those eyes. Or watch out for your workload and cut yourself some slack!

- If you are bored, play, get creative, have fun.

This is all about meeting your own needs. Tapping into that ego state and showing up as your very own loving and nurturing parent.

Set boundaries

Get clear on your values and needs and set healthy, respectful boundaries with the people in your life. Set boundaries with yourself, too; stick to commitments you make for yourself and show up with compassion, time and time again. Prove to yourself you can rely on you.

Stop trying to please everyone else

You are not that little person any more who had to hustle about meeting everyone else's needs and making sure others were happy. Write a new script. Your role on this planet is not to serve everyone else but yourself. Being a people-pleaser is a sure-fire way to build resentment while simultaneously dismissing your own needs. Even if you don't feel it, begin to prioritise the things you need and want — your belief that you deserve this will follow.

Prioritise your needs

Get clear on what you need and make it a non-negotiable priority. Yes, this might feel uncomfortable at first. And that's okay. Little-you will thank you for it!

Speak to yourself like a loving parent, or an adult at least

Switch ego states out of the critical parent, out of the adaptive child. Speak to yourself with love, compassion and kindness. Speak to yourself how you would speak to someone you love. Go back to pages 14–30 about the inner critic if you need a refresher.

Play!

Tap into your free child ego state by:

- allowing yourself to have fun

- getting creative and making a mess

- laughing, making room in your day for things that aren't serious, and not taking yourself so seriously

- moving your body

- dancing

- being curious, rather than defensive or closed

- making mistakes

- forgiving yourself.

Use affirmations

Here are some lovely affirmations you might like to incorporate into your inner-child work. Maybe when you notice yourself slipping into ruminating on the past, dwelling on regrets, being hard on yourself or feeling vulnerable, you could read and repeat these to yourself.

INNER CHILD AFFIRMATIONS:

♡ I am seen

♡ I let go of regret & guilt

♡ I am safe

♡ I am not broken

♡ I am loveable

♡ I deserve kindness & care

♡ I let go of wishing the past was different & embrace my power in the present

Here's a tool to try: write a letter to your past-self. Think of
a time in your life when you were struggling and could have
desperately used some words of compassion, wisdom and
love. Write a letter from 'present-day, compassionate, adult
you', to this 'past inner-child you', like this:

Dear me,
   I know things are ~~a bit tough~~ a struggle for
you right now. It's a real rough patch.
   I promise you that you will get through this...
You'll even learn some valuable things about
yourself - one of which is that you are so much
stronger than you realise.
Hang in there - things are going to get better.
                                    Love, me. ♡

Try a visualisation

A final tool for this section is the 'inner child visualisation'. You'll find
the guide and script for this below. In this visualisation, the 'inner
child' can be a younger version of yourself at any age. It doesn't
have to be in childhood; maybe this is just a version of you from a
year ago when times were tough. Maybe this is you as a teenager.
Whatever speaks to you. A tip: you could record yourself reading
this script aloud, taking your time for deep breaths and pauses to

soak it all in. Then, you can lie back somewhere cosy, pop in your headphones and guide yourself through this visualisation.

A final note: when asked to picture a younger version of you or a version of you who is struggling, be gentle here and ease in. Ideally, don't pick a time of immense trauma right off the bat — you don't want to trigger yourself or go too deep too fast. Experiment first with a tricky-but-not-too-threatening time in your life and see how that feels. As with any tool in this book, if it doesn't feel right or it brings up too much emotion for you to manage, you can pause and skip the exercise. You could work with a therapist or counsellor around anything that feels triggering. Look after yourself here.

EXERCISE

Take a seat somewhere comfortable, or lie down. Take a few nourishing deep breaths here, directing your inhale deep into your belly. Focus on slowing your breathing, perhaps allowing your exhale to lengthen out, longer than your inhale. Notice the support beneath you, shifting your awareness to the parts of your body that are in contact with the surface under you. Allow yourself to relax and sink in, feeling held and supported here. Close your eyes.

Now you are going to bring to mind your inner child; for this visualisation, you will picture a version of yourself at any moment in your past when times were tough and you were struggling. Maybe this is you in childhood, maybe it is a time during your teen years, or perhaps it is a more recent version of you.

Visualise this past-self. Where were you? Who was, or wasn't, around you in that moment? Picture yourself in a scene where things were a bit rough. Notice what this version of you looks like. How did you appear to be feeling? What were you thinking about?

Now visualise a current-day you; this version of you looks compassionate and loving. Imagine this loving-you is walking into the scene with past-you. Picture a warm, glowing golden light surrounding the loving and present version of yourself. Take a few deep belly breaths here and bathe in the warm healing light.

See this loving-you approaching your past-self. They meet. Perhaps loving-you wraps your past-self in a warm embrace, a hug, or a hand on the shoulder. You see this healing golden light begin to surround your past-self, covering and enveloping them in warmth and a protective glow.

Now offer these words to your past-self:

You were doing the best you could at
the time with what you knew.

You have always been worthy of love, respect and belonging.

I can re-parent myself by allowing myself compassion, speaking
to myself with kindness and meeting my own needs.

I can set and uphold boundaries for myself in the present.

My past-self, hurts and decisions no longer
have to be carried by me in the present.

Finally, let's tune into our needs. Imagine asking the past version of yourself, 'What do you need?' Now wait. Breathe deeply into your belly and just observe what comes up. Maybe this past-you needed to feel safe, maybe they needed someone to talk to, maybe they needed a hug, a nice cup of tea . . . whatever it is that comes up, you may give this to yourself now. You can meet this need. Step back a little, and visualise this past version of yourself looking more content, shrouded in protective light and healing.

It's time now to come back to the present, stepping fully into your current-day, loving self. Begin by simply tuning back into your breath, noticing each inhalation and exhalation. Notice your body, the sensations, the surface beneath you. Tune into the sounds around you. The smells. Observe the light filtering through your closed eyelids.

Slowly open your eyes and sit up. Rub your feet on the floor, telling yourself, 'I am here now. I am safe.' Finally, proceed with something helpful that meets your need. Maybe you can offer yourself some kind words, a break for a cuppa, or a gentle stroll.

There is no desired outcome from this visualisation. It's okay if it felt tricky, or you weren't sure what past-you needed. Don't give up on the practice. Try again another time, extending compassion to any struggling version of yourself, and inviting yourself to identify and meet your own needs.

Imagine asking the past version of yourself, 'What do you need?' Now wait. Breathe deeply into your belly and just observe what comes up.

Protection Parts

When I think about self-sabotage, anxiety, worry, perfectionism, people-pleasing, procrastination, self-doubt, having your walls up — almost anything like this that we do as humans — I like to frame it under the concept of 'protection parts'.

What is a protection part?

A protection part is a part of you that came to exist as a way to protect you and get you through a hard time in your life. This behaviour, response or way of thinking was completely adaptive at the time. It got you through and it helped you do what you needed to do to survive (literally or figuratively). As a result of this, we often unconsciously continue the pattern of the protection part. It becomes the way we reflexively respond in the present. Often our protection parts develop in childhood or our early years, or as a result of a trauma or an incredibly hard time in our lives. Let's take people-pleasing, for example.

> Meet your protection part: the people-pleaser. Maybe you
> want to give it a name, like Penelope. Perhaps as a child your
> parents shut down any of the difficult behaviours or emotions
> you displayed. It wasn't acceptable in your house to talk back,
> question rules, cry, hold your own boundaries or get angry.
> You learnt that to be accepted and feel safe in your family you
> had to put on a face and act a certain way. You learnt that by
> pleasing your parents, things ran smoothly in your world. And
> so developed Penelope. Now, as an adult, Penelope often
> kicks you out of the driver's seat and takes the wheel. Any time
> you feel like someone doesn't like you, or you worry you are

being judged, Penelope springs into action, frantically trying to please others. Penelope got you through your childhood years. She was adaptive. She was very intelligent, actually.

Now meet another protection part: the worrier. As a teenager, your parents separated and you went through some turbulent friendship changes. You became fixated on what could go wrong in your relationships and the worrier stepped in to protect you. The worrier sat front and centre, presenting you with all the possible things that might happen, trying to read people's minds and asking 'what if . . . ?' at every turn in order to preempt any more problems and save you from heartache.

How can you make peace with your protection parts?

The protection parts in the above example, along with all the others, came about for a reason. They were seeking to keep you safe, and they were extremely useful at the time. Only now they seem to be restricting your full potential, holding you back when your true self is dying to burst free. Now, as an adult, you need to do this:

- Become aware of your protection parts. In other words, get to know the ways you act in order to keep yourself safe.

- Acknowledge and name these protection parts with compassion.

- Remind yourself you are here and it is now. You are not back in the past. 'Okay Penelope, I see you there. But it isn't 1996 any more — I've got this.'

- Thank your protection part for its service and remain in the driver's seat, calming yourself in the present and acting in ways that support your growth.

In this book, you are learning about lots of ways you might try to protect yourself — there are so many different protection parts you might uncover. A key reminder is to love all of these parts of yourself, rather than meeting them with resistance, shame or judgement. Remind yourself that they developed with the very best intentions for you. Hold space to acknowledge that at one time these protection parts were the very best defence you had. Now you know better, you can do better. Now you know more, you can be more.

A part of the work in building self-love is befriending our shadows. By shedding light on these parts of ourselves and by getting to know them, we can starve them of the judgement and shame that they thrive on, creating space for compassion, understanding and even acceptance.

> A part of the work in building self-love is befriending our shadows.

Summary

- It's crucial that you keep your own watering can topped up through self-care practices.

- There are many bite-sized practices that you can incorporate into your day that can help to build your resilience and wellbeing.

- Affirmations are a lovely way to feed your brain messages of love and compassion.

- If you struggle to believe or take on an affirmation, you may be experiencing cognitive dissonance. Make your affirmations work for you by making them believable.

- We can all nurture and heal our inner child through reparenting work, meeting our own needs and treating ourselves with love and compassion.

- We all have protection parts that develop in order to keep us safe and get us through hard times.

- We can acknowledge and hold compassion and gratitude for these protection parts while consciously choosing to remain present and in the driver's seat, choosing new responses going forward.

Go forward. Keep showing up for you. And give yourself the grace to be totally and utterly imperfectly human.

A Final Word

You made it — you finished the book!

First, let's just take a moment to pause and soak it all in. Congratulate yourself. You showed up for you and you took a huge step in the journey to being your best self.

Now what? I want you to take some time to integrate all the things you have read and learnt. Not every single thing in this book will speak to you, and that's okay. Take the parts that felt in alignment and run with those. You don't need to go from here and work on all of the life-changing ideas in this book at once — that would be totally overwhelming and make anyone want to crawl into the foetal position! Remember that key thread of compassion. It might be useful to start with just one thing, or maybe a small handful of things, and begin to intentionally incorporate them into your life.

Some of you will go from here and focus in on boundaries. Some of you will be on a mission to calm and regulate your nervous systems. Others will be off for a mindful cup of tea. Maybe you're going to go for a walk and leave the dishes on the bench? Whatever it is that you do from here, I applaud you! Once you feel like you've made progress with your first focus, you come on back to this book, skim over the parts you dog-eared and choose another area.

Becoming your best self is an ongoing work in progress — as are we all. It's a journey and it is ever-evolving. Each and every one of us does the best we can with what we know. My hope for you is that you go forward from here armed with a whole smorgasbord of new information and insights to help you become the best version of you, and that you do that with compassion.

Becks

First published in 2023

Text and illustrations © Rebekah Ballagh, 2023

Note: Client names and some details have been changed to protect the privacy
of individuals.

Allen & Unwin
Level 2, 10 College Hill
Auckland 1011, New Zealand
Phone: (64 9) 377 3800

Email: info@allenandunwin.com
Web: www.allenandunwin.co.nz

83 Alexander Street
Crows Nest NSW 2065, Australia
Phone: (61 2) 8425 0100

A catalogue record for this book is available
from the National Library of New Zealand

ISBN 978 1 99100 601 1

Design by Kate Barraclough

Set in 10.5/16pt Untitled Sans light and Ivy Mode
Printed and bound in China by C&C Printing Co. Ltd
10 9 8 7 6 5 4 3 2 1

MIX
Paper | Supporting
responsible forestry
FSC
www.fsc.org
FSC® C008047